1

# Fundraising Your Way:

## How To Conduct An Effective And Profitable Product Fundraiser

Authored by Jesse L. Carter

This publication is designed to provide accurate and authoritative information in regard to the subject matter covered (nonprofit product fundraising).  It is sold with the understanding that the author is not engaged in rendering legal, accounting, or other professional service.  If legal advice or other expert assistance is required, the services of a competent professional person should be sought.

# Fundraising Your Way:

## How To Conduct An Effective And Profitable Product Fundraiser

**About The Author** – Jesse Carter is President of Carter Resource Development. He is Founder of Profit Quests Fundraising (ProfitQuests.com) and FundraisingYourWay.com, two national online fundraising companies offering fundraising advice and assistance to nonprofit organizations. Jesse offers nonprofit groups, organizations, churches, ministries, clubs and associations many fundraising resources, tips, ideas and fundraising products.

His nonprofit experience extends over 26 years and ranges from managing and directing major multi-million dollar capital campaigns of colleges and charities to working with church youth and scouting groups raising just enough to send their kids to camp.

His company, Carter Resource Development, has a particular interest in assisting small to large nonprofit organizations in their efforts to build their support base. Over his career, he has helped thousands of nonprofit groups raise millions of dollars for their benefit.

Jesse is a publisher, author, entrepreneur, consultant, business owner and has been featured as a regular expert guest speaker on syndicated fundraising shows. He is an accomplished Million Dollar Sales professional.

He has been a member of the two top fundraising industry organizations - Association of Fund Raising Distributors And Suppliers (AFRDS) and Association of Fundraising Professionals (AFP) over the years.

Jesse also offers consulting services and development strategy for several national nonprofit organizations, as well as, national direct sales companies that desire to integrate fundraising into their sales efforts.

He holds a Bachelor of Science and a Master of Science degree from the University Of Louisiana – Monroe.

Some of his charitable work has involved serving as Executive Director of a few charities, Senior Director with the Boy Scouts of America, Youth Pastor, Development Director and participating on numerous Board Of Directors.

Jesse is married to his wife Karen of twenty six years.

**Fundraising Your Way:**
**How To Conduct An Effective And Profitable Product Fundraiser**


## Table Of Contents

# Acknowledgements

To my lovely and brilliant wife Karen who has seen all types of my fundraising jobs and career moves and has traveled with me all across the country for me to do so. She has worked alongside me many times to edit materials, type reports, create funding packets and put together proposals.

She has helped with my efforts assisting clients too many times to count. In a pinch, she's been known to work as an auction treasurer, ticket dispenser, grant writer, Executive Director, speaker and even as the Chair of a Boy Scout District Popcorn Drive.

Thanks also to my daughter Kelsey Carter for the artistic design on many of the pages. She has a gift of creating things that are totally unique and that has never been done before.

The "popcorn people" you'll see here are a totally new idea of hers. I've seen her as a child create unbelievable toys with just some paper clips, tape, old screws and sticky notes. She is in high school at this writing so the sky is the limit with her creative and artistic abilities.

# Introduction

Allow me to explain WHY this book will guide you in starting your organization down the right path to achieving success with your first... or perhaps next product fundraiser.

I have been involved with fundraising efforts for many years since 1986 when I started my professional fundraising career as a District Executive at a Boy Scout District in North Little Rock, Arkansas. Up until that point, because of my natural shyness, I would have never considered "asking someone for money". I was an Eagle Scout and had a rich Scouting background as a youth, so I saw the challenge to learn to be a true executive in the scouting profession.

I hope to make this book as conversational as possible, but forgive me if my scientific nature kicks in. You see I have two degrees in Geology and it is natural for me to be precise with an analytical approach while applying features to get the results that I'm looking for. Fundraising is not a science, but I'll get you as close to it as possible.

This will be to your advantage, I hope, as I give you the exact details which you'll need in recreating what I've successfully achieved with other nonprofit groups I've helped.

This book will give you my knowledge and experience over the years in helping clients and organizations across the country. Even though there is a lot of information and details, do not let it overwhelm you since you will have it to refer to again and again.

I also created an online fundraising website in 1999 called ProfitQuests.com and a newly created website called FundraisingYourWay.com to help groups that could not afford fundraising consultation costs. There you will find additional fundraising tools, fundraising forms, ideas, articles and other free fundraising information.

If you are working with any Fundraising Company or Distributor, this book will help you be more effective as you work with them and cut your time to implement your fundraising campaign.

I plan to give you tremendous insight into running an effective product fundraiser. I find that it is better to give you as much information as possible rather than to not give you enough to get the job done.  You are welcome to use only those areas that apply to your group's specific fundraising efforts.

For those who have already conducted a product fundraiser before, I hope this reliable information adds to your knowledge base and perhaps gives you some ideas to make your next effort even more successful.

This book will be a very hard read if you try to read it through and absorb it all in one setting.  Rather, I suggest you read it by skimming over it all and get a big picture of what's inside.  Use it like a "cookbook" and decide what particular "fundraising recipe" you would like to try out.

Once you've selected your fundraising "cookbook" recipe, it will allow you to decide where your focus should be best placed.

Did you choose a poor fundraising product last year and need to fine tune the selection of this year's product?  Then you should start with the section on **Selecting Your Product**.

Are you inexperienced at recruiting your Fundraising Team or have done a weak job in the past?  Then you should go right to the **Securing Your Fundraising Campaign Leadership** section which will show you how to create the most dynamic team of workers possible.

I think you get the picture.  However, if you want to really absorb this book and become the expert, by all means read and study it as much as possible.  Perhaps, you could even split up some of the sections among your Fundraising Committee Members to become the "expert" on that particular section.  Then get ready for some lively and informative Fundraising Committee Meetings.

# Getting Started

Why do nonprofit organizations do fundraisers?  Or a better question is…
Why do we need to do fundraisers in order to help the organization we're
involved with?  Well, charities and nonprofit organizations need funds to carry
out their mission.  It's really that simple!

A large majority of American consumers believe that product fundraising,
which is what this book is about, is a very important way for organizations,
schools and groups to raise funds.  Most will purchase at least one product
during the year if asked.

If your nonprofit organization is like most organizations out there, the need for
fundraising is greater than ever before and your nonprofit group will need to
secure additional sources of income at an ever increasing pace.

What are some of the things your organization has a need for?

- Mission trips or supporting charities in other countries?
- A new building for your campus or worship center?
- Athletic programs and sports supplies?
- Annual operational expenses?
- Employee salaries?
- Musical instruments?
- Playground equipment?
- Clothes or Food Pantry Offerings?
- Medical and charitable supplies?
- Annual Event or Gathering Expenses?
- Perhaps an important need for your organization we've not mentioned?

Certainly traditional fundraisers like Car Washes and Bake Sale Fundraisers
offer limited results.  They require a much greater outlay of energy and
manpower than what will be required with most product fundraisers which sell
items through the use of colorful pre-sale sales brochures and flyers, through
online shopping websites or with on-the-spot sales.

Now, let's not kid ourselves into thinking we aren't required to sell anything or
ask our members and supporters to buy anything.

Notice that I use the words "sell" and "sale". That's what It's all about... selling a product and making money from the sale.

A majority of Americans purchase products to support organizations and schools. The number one reason why people don't buy a fundraising product is because they were not asked to buy or in other words, "they are not approached and sold" a product.

Selling and sales have been one of the most noble of professions, but often times those not familiar with selling will have stereotypical images come to mind that cast a bad light on those who do enjoy selling or make a living selling as a chosen profession.

However, in our nonprofit world, we are not talking about professional salespeople. We're talking about individuals working in a charitable endeavor and offering items for sale so that their nonprofit organization can use the profits generated to accomplish a financial goal which has been set. Money raised naturally helps fund their mission.

Every year booster clubs alone raise tens of thousands of dollars each for their cause. This turns in to tens of millions raised annually by these clubs nationwide.

The Association of Fund Raising Distributors and Suppliers (AFRDS) has data showing where nonprofit organizations of all shapes and sizes raise nearly $1.7 billion each year. It also states in one of their recent announcements, "The vast majority of Americans (80%) agree that "product fundraising is an important financial resource for America's schools and youth programs".

I've heard it said from some fundraising professionals that you should not focus on the "dollars and cents" aspects of what a group needs, but rather on the great philanthropic efforts and works which the group is doing. I say that you need both. You need to deliver a compelling story of why you need to raise funds while allowing your supporters to know exactly how much money you need to raise in order to meet your goals.

There are all sorts of reasons why groups use product sales to raise funds. These reasons include money for uniforms, playgrounds, out-of-town travel costs, new equipment, competition expenses, facilities expansion, special purchases, tournaments and hosting of special events.

Any of these could be your "compelling story". And the cost of achieving this will be what you need to raise.

Your fundraising campaign involves two distinct groups of people as it unfolds. These two essential groups WILL determine the outcome of your fundraiser.

First, you need a <u>Fundraising Team</u> made up of those members within your organization who have a desire to participate and help raise funds. I call these key volunteers... 'Fundraising Team Members'. Their focus is first on raising money and secondly of achieving their personal fundraising (and thereby the group) goal.

Secondly, you have your <u>Supporters</u>. These are customers who focus on your group's financial support needs. They want to know why the money is needed and how they can help you raise those funds by buying your products.

Probably THE biggest challenge in fundraising is that, more than likely, people new to fundraising are afraid to ask their neighbors, relatives and friends for support or to sell them anything.

These new fundraising volunteers begin to create zones of discomfort for themselves where they find it difficult to cross, even if it's for a good cause.

Did you know that about four out of every five people will support at least one fundraiser during any given year? Also, in a recent statement from the AFRDS it announced, "More than three-quarters of all Americans (76%) are comfortable spending up to $20 per fundraising occasion".

So people you approach are more comfortable being asked to support your cause by buying a product than you might at first believe. Just don't be shy about asking.

Perhaps the simplest way to look at this is to ask yourself, "How would I like to be approached about buying a product that helps support our organization?" If you wouldn't mind buying a fundraising product, then it should be OK, right?

Actually, most people love to be asked to help a worthy cause. By participating, they become an integral part of something worthy of their support.

You simply have to present them with what you are offering. You simply have to ASK them to support your efforts.

Basically, you are presenting to them products offered through a reputable Fundraising Company that they might want to purchase. Supporters simply buy an item On-The-Spot or they can review a sales brochure or flyer then choose to participate by buying or not. When they do purchase an item, you share in the profits from the sale.

A well quoted scripture verse, Luke 11:9-10, says it most precisely, "And I say unto you, Ask, and it shall be given you; seek, and ye shall find; knock, and it shall be opened unto you. For everyone that asketh receiveth; and he that seeketh findeth; and to him that knocketh it shall be opened."

The meaning is quite clear. Don't worry about someone disliking what you have to present - just decide to tell them about it. You probably will be pleasantly surprised that many will want to learn more about the great benefits your organization provides to the community and then become more involved themselves.

Later on I want to tell you some of my Rules For Success which I've learned over the years. Each of these is absolutely necessary to vault from a lackluster effort to a remarkably successful fundraising campaign. For now, let's start with the basics of establishing some Accountability factors along with Public Relations and Publicity.

As you read these sections, you may want to be thinking of someone within your organization to head them up. By all means, share the workload.

# Accountability, Public Relations And Sales Publicity

## Accountability

As you get started in planning your product fundraiser and setting out on the right path, it is a good idea to notify the public of your plans. I would advise you to first check with your state and local municipality whether it is necessary to register your nonprofit organization offering a legitimate fundraiser taking place in your community.

Some local governing boards or municipalities require nonprofits to Officially Register their fundraising program. Why? Well, quite frankly it is because the number of scams taking place on behalf of charities. Your efforts are of course not a scam, but why not head off any citizen concerns by letting others know what you are doing. This is especially true if you are conducting door-to-door sales.

It is always a good idea to notify residents in some way or to have a way for them to call the authorities to determine if your nonprofit group is officially conducting a fundraiser in your community. This is all about legitimate communications with potential supporters and will certainly cut down on any confusion or complaints. It just makes good sense to always be seen on the up-and-up.

## Public Relations

I would make it a practice, as a part of your Public Relations campaign anyway, to alert the Better Business Bureau, Chamber Of Commerce, Sherriff's Office, City Police and Mayor's Office as a courtesy to the public. Fill out any official paperwork as needed and include a brief, one page Press Release.

Your efforts in communicating to area officials way may also unexpectedly open some doors to promote your fundraiser to its employees, member base or citizenry.

Your one to two page Press Release should be double spaced and cover the five W's of who, what, when, where, why and how. You might also want to include a brief quote from a prominent member of your community who is connected with your effort as this will draw the attention of the reader.

It might appear something like...

SUBJECT: Major Fundraiser Now Open To The Public

DATE: January 20, 2020
WHO: ABC Nonprofit Organization
EFFECTIVE: For Immediate Release
KEY CONTACT: Mr. John Doe, (XXX) 555-5555, johnjohndoe@doe.org

The ABC NONPROFIT ORGANIZATION is conducting a new product fundraiser now available to members of our community and supporters in our area. Our Honorary Chair, Mayor Jones, states, "I would hope that every citizen in our community would want to support the ABC Nonprofit Organization to reach its goal of $X00,000."

It's such a totally unique and phenomenal fundraising program, that we've asked all interested consumers in our community to participate. We believe you will be excited about securing your very own _____Give The Product Fundraiser Name Here_____.

Describe the product(s) here in one sentence. Retail Prices for the _Product Names Here_ range from _$10?_ to _$20?_ and we receive a large portion of the proceeds.

Our annual sale extends from _____Date_____ and ends on _____Date_____.

This special fundraiser is being offered to help us fulfill our mission of _____state reason here_____ which is much needed in these difficult economic times.

Your support is appreciated. For more information you may go to our website www.ABCNonprofitGroupname.org, see us on Facebook or call us at (xxx) xxx – xxxx and we will have one of our team members reach out to you.

## Sales Publicity

Promotion of your campaign should take place before, during and after your fundraising product sale. Ideally, you should appoint one individual who will handle this important part of your fundraiser.

There are two areas to consider when determining how to proceed with your sales publicity. They are: 1) Size of your fundraiser and 2) Involvement with the public.

*The size of your fundraiser* may determine if you need a managed publicity effort or are even large enough to need a Publicity Chair. For instance, if your club has 10 to 20 Fundraising Team Members then the only publicity you will need can be handled easily by the Campaign Chair since the job should not be too difficult for one person to "get the word out".

Generally, I don't recommend that the Fundraising Campaign Chair handle more than their own job, but for small fundraising efforts it's not necessary to recruit another person just to handle the limited scope of your publicity efforts. If say, your group is a small Boy Scout Troop, then you may assign someone on the Troop Committee who already has this job to reach out to the public.

For larger groups of 40 members or more, you should appoint a Publicity Chair to be in charge of reaching out to the community about your fundraiser. Large schools should definitely have someone in charge of publicity. This person should be proactive and not simply respond to inquiries made from the outside. Remember, the more you promote your fundraiser, the more people will know about it and be inclined to participate with you.

*Involvement with the public* simply refers to how active you will be in reaching out beyond your own membership. For instance, if your church youth group plans to just contact its own church membership and not reach out into the community, then you will not need much of a publicity effort... except for the pastor to make a few quick comments to the congregation or place an article in the church newsletter or on the church website.

Alternatively, I knew of a club that promoted a seasonal Pecan Fundraising Sale before the Fall Holidays which had to conduct a large scale communication effort to establish interest in the community. They definitely needed a Publicity Chair and a big push to drive people toward their sale.

In any event, your publicity effort should include a few principles for success:

1. Create a name or theme for your fundraising sale that gives everyone pause to take notice and perhaps consider supporting your fundraising sale. Make sure you emphasize the reason for your fundraiser.

2. Post the Goal Thermometer in as many public spots as possible. This will certainly draw attention to your funding needs. Post these in newsletters, on websites, outdoor signs, in group's social media page, local newspaper, and radio station websites.

3. Make announcements ahead of time using various media including online social media. Be consistent to reach out daily for two weeks prior to your sale and during your sale timeframe. Try an automated calling system or have a small team of volunteers call all Fundraising Team Members and remind them of the sale timeframe and final turn-in-date.

4. State the Final End Date, products being sold, and some information on how to contact your organization (website address, email, phone number, and contact name).

## Bad Publicity Or Sales Techniques

Any good evaluation of publicity or sales techniques will also steer you away from efforts that just don't work very well. Here are a few bad technique examples:

1. Simply passing out flyers or sales brochures and expecting people to be self-inspired to participate and buy a product on their own. *Hint: You must ask them personally to buy – it's that face-to-face or person-to-person advantage which you must actually use.*

2. Being exclusionary by accepting only cash as a means of payment. *Hint: You must accept as many payment methods as you can – try PayPal Payment Processing for Nonprofits where they take all types of payments and it's free to sign-up. Also, look into Square.com for free credit card swipers.*

3. Make people feel guilty about not supporting your efforts. *Hint: People giving to a worthy cause want to be inspired in some way… like they are making a difference. Feeling guilty will make them 'uninspired' and not want to help you out again in the future.*

4. Parents take a sales order form to work and just leave it on their desk for people to fill out. *Hint: There needs to be an immediate "call to action" by*

*asking co-workers face-to-face to help your child reach his or her goal. And just for the record, adults will buy more products from other adult co-workers asking as opposed to a child who takes the order form around the office and pressures someone to buy only one item out of guilt. Adults are much more likely to tell a young person to "come back when I've got the money" rather than adult co-workers which would be embarrassing, signaling they are too broke to buy a $12 tub of cookie dough.*

<u>Publicity Sales Tactics To Use</u>

1. Consider limiting your fundraiser to once per year. Let people know… "when it's over it's over till next year, so get yours today"… "we only have this sale once per year so contact us before the end of next week"… "turn your purchase into a gift for your friends and family just in time for the holidays".

2. If possible, personalize your products by printing your organization's name, logo and website on the product. Some candy bar companies and sauce companies are great about placing the group's name, photo and website where anyone using the product can identify with and find out more ways of helping the group.

3. When you first approach your customers and ask them for a sale you may want to give them several "referral slips" which allows them to refer their friends and neighbors to your fundraiser. The referral slip will have a place to put their name and phone number on it and may offer an incentive like, "receive a free candle if 4 other friends help us out and decide to buy" using the referral slip.

4. Offer a 'free raffle' or 'giveaway' as featured on a postcard you've created (*see Microsoft Office Templates online*) and hand to every customer who buys two or more products. They fill out the postcard with their contact information and you take it to a "ticket pot" to be pulled from later. Offer a Flat Screen TV to adults… an expensive coffee maker to adults if you are selling coffee products… an iPod if teenagers are involved selling candy or treats… or any type of specific item that fits with your customer type and/or product being sold. Typically, most supporters will buy just one item, because they will "feel guilty NOT buying 'something'" from their relative or neighbors son or daughter. Give anybody a chance to get something extra, and then they will likely buy more. Personally, I wouldn't go past two or three items to help the supporter reach their threshold.

5. Place your fundraising sales website (or your group website at the very least) using a sticker on any product which will be delivered to your customers once the sales campaign is over. If they like your product, then they can order more… which will increase sales. This is especially true if you have some sort of ecommerce Fundraising Product Website like those seen at FreeWebFundraiser.com which offers fundraising products for sale all year long.

Place labels on "instant sale" items like candy bars, single serve coffee packs, snacks or treats for anyone who likes the product to call and order more. You sell more products from a repeat customer who is already convinced of the value of your product and will gladly purchase again. This has doubled or even quadrupled the expected sales for many groups.

6. Of course, you should add your fundraising campaign specifics to your YouTube (youtube.com) account and a blog (blogger.com) as long as you have the means to broadcast the links by email messaging or social media posting.

7. Offer several locations where people can purchase items during your sales campaign. For instance, have members of your fundraising team conduct your sale at a nursing home, large school or college campus, and supermarket the first week. The second week, have fundraising team members located at a retirement village, major shopping mall, or city hall. The third and final week have members of your team at a sports event, major grocery store and large open park.

Think of other areas where there will be buyers. Perhaps VA Clinics, Senior Citizen Centers, outdoor farmers markets, city hall/police stations, civic centers, fuel travel centers, department stores, etc.

8. Create an 8 ½ X 5 ½ Local Merchant Coupon Sheet with discounts by local merchants where each Fundraising Team Member can hand to each person they approach. I would personally only offer it to those who purchase as a "Thank You" incentive, but you may decide to give a Coupon Sheet for anyone who is approached whether they buy or not. On this sheet you will want to have your own coupon for 10% off any item purchased during your next fundraising event or to go online and purchase items for direct delivery to their home. Sell these advertising spots to merchants for extra revenue toward the campaign goal.

9. When posting information on your group's blog or website, be sure to allow readers to share posts through their own social media outlets. You might

want to provide the "forwarding button", "like us", "sharing link" or embedded link of the page which explains your fundraising team effort.

## Social Media Publicity

As a part of any modern publicity effort you should use online social media to get the word out. Your group should secure any or all of these social media outlets like Facebook (facebook.com), Google+ (http://plus.google.com), Twitter (twitter.com), LinkedIn (linkedin.com), MySpace (myspace.com) and Google Buzz (google.com/buzz). You can also use TotalSnap (totalsnap.com) or Homestead (Homestead.com).

You may assume that many of your Fundraising Team Members have one or more of these social outlets available personally. This is the perfect way to communicate with them over the course of the campaign. Twitter is much more effective as a way to instantly communicate with Fundraising Team Members with important messages or as a means to inspire them as they work the campaign.

These methods should not be exclusive of sending notices by email, text or direct telephone calls to communicate with your team. The larger your group is, the less likely you can insure everybody will receive timely messages through social media only.

It's easy to create a social media page for your group to alert your workers and supporters, but it is far more effective if it is used by supportive individuals to reach out to family and friends.

A personal social media site is very effective for any Fundraising Team Member to reach their personal sales goal by contacting family and friends and asking for their help. An alternative would be to create their own Microsite like on TotalSnap.com or Pinterest.com.

Social Media is a very good way to communicate with the community, but especially through your Fundraising Team Members and to those they will contact. See the section on Email Campaign and adapt for your Social Media message.

# Rules For Success

Every organization wants to achieve success in reaching their fundraising goal. To truly reach your success threshold you need to implement some key success principles within your plan of action.

Over the years I've uncovered several top Rules Of Success. Allow me to list them in order from start to finish and then discuss them in more detail later.

1. Choose a Campaign Chair from within your organization who will "make the fundraiser happen".

2. The organization should "take possession" of the fundraiser and make the fundraiser a priority.

3. You MUST set a firm "fundraising goal" and announce it to your community. This makes it serious enough for everyone to see.

4. All Key Leaders and Fundraising Team Members should "lead by example" and be the first to buy the products BEFORE the official kickoff takes place. Implement this one simple rule and you will be guaranteed to have successful sale on some scale.

5. Adhere to a "strict campaign timeline".

Let's look at each of these a little more closely!

*Choose a Campaign Chair from within your organization who will "make the fundraiser happen"* – Any responsible organization will recruit or appoint a dedicated person just for the specific fundraising campaign. There should be someone in charge who will "make the fundraiser happen".

Ask this individual for a minimal, but specific timeframe to get the job done. Have your CEO and VP or similar top two leaders personally make an appointment and ask this person face-to-face to consider the Fundraising Campaign Chair position.

Being asked by the top two leaders face-to-face, sets the atmosphere for how important this fundraiser is to the organization. Mention to your potential Campaign Chair that you plan to achieve the goal by having the absolute best person to head it up.  This quickly explains to them there is a lot riding on their shoulders if they decide to accept the challenge.  In essence, you are asking them to "make it happen".

When asking, you should have a typed job description on hand with a timeframe of what they are being asked to commit to.  I have created some job description sheets and have included them at the end of this book for your use when approaching your recruit.

***The organization should "take possession" of the fundraiser and make the fundraiser a priority*** – Your fundraising campaign can't be a passive effort put forth on a whim.  You must seize the moment and take possession to achieve your fundraising goal.  Without taking possession of the fundraiser, it just won't be successful.

You've heard people make comments like... "Well, if it happens, it happens" or "We don't need too much money, so if we get a few sales, then it's better than nothing".  You may have heard other similar statements showing an unworthy effort.

Too many times I have seen an organization or school with a funding shortfall add a product fundraiser in desperation to help them reach their normal funding goal.

When this desperation becomes apparent; typically, one of their members frantically suggests attempting an "easy" fundraiser they've been told about, which will raise a lot of money and without much volunteer effort expended.

So the group's leader, who is already tired from the many fundraisers they've had to do, says "go for it" and hopes that it will all fall into place without much action needed.  This leads the leaders to not take the new fundraiser seriously enough and just expecting it to "happen".

As with any effective effort, you must take possession of the fundraiser and put some serious effort into it.  You want to succeed right?  Then there should be nothing less than a total success oriented movement to make it occur.

When you go out to the public and ask them to purchase items, you don't want to be seen as being less than 100% on board in presenting it to them.

We all know after dining at a delightful restaurant how we are inspired to tell others about how good it was?  What if lots of people were doing the same thing?  You would expect for that restaurant to become a huge success.

This same success principle applies to reaching out to others concerning your fundraising campaign.  You simply must have as many inspired people involved as possible.

As you are "taking possession" of your Fundraising Product Campaign, you will need to show your enthusiasm and positive excitement about your fundraiser.  This will be a part of the main ingredients to ensure success for your group.

If volunteers or leaders from your group are not "possession" oriented, then there will be no word-of-mouth promotion of the fundraiser either.  You have to have everybody engaged and excited about what you are trying to accomplish... reaching your fundraising goal!

*You MUST set a firm "fundraising goal" and announce it to your community* – After showing you are serious about raising money for your project or mission, you must set the mark by establishing a fundraising goal for your group to reach.  You'll want to indicate that you expect everyone to seriously help in the achievement of that goal.

Winners working toward any worthwhile endeavor, on every level, are "goal oriented" and your efforts in making your fundraiser a success are no exception.

Keep in mind, the more "goal oriented" your Fundraising Team Members are for both their own personal goals, as well as the overall group campaign goal, the better you will achieve the profits your group desires.

You should always do the best job possible in explaining "why" you are conducting this fundraiser.

You may choose from two types of Goals: 1) Number Of Products Sold or 2) Money Raised.  You will want to use a Thermometer Goal Chart to keep track of either.  There are two types of these placed at the end of the book.

A goal should include a dollar amount and brief description of what you are raising money for.  An example would be, "ABC Nonprofit is seeking to raise

$20,000 for our annual 'Help A Kid In Need' Rally utilizing the AAA Triple Scented Candle Company Sale now through October 30th."

This shows the actual dollar amount while explaining what the money will be used for and how you will achieve it by selling a specific product by a certain date. Placing your Goal Thermometer near your explanation will add to the visual effects of what you are attempting to accomplish.

Be sure when you talk about "money raised", it should be the actual profit made. This would be the retail price offered to your customers minus the cost of the product (wholesale cost plus shipping and handling expenses) from your fundraising company.

You may even elect to have a suggested minimum "personal goal" for your Fundraising Team Members which they are expected to achieve.

For instance, for a grade school student involved with a Candle Fundraiser, you may ask them and their parents to sell 3 candles each. If every student does that, you could raise a significant amount of money.

You may also have different levels of goals, that if reached, they achieve some type of incentive. There is a section in the book called Sales Incentives And Prizes that explains more on this subject.

As a side note, there is only one thing that trumps an achievable goal for helping your group sell the most it can… and that's "who" is doing the asking? You see, most supporters tend to buy from "who is doing the asking" rather than on the worthiness of supporting the cause alone.


So, that's why…

Grandparents are asked by their grandkids and tend to say "yes",
or
Favorite office buddies are asked by other co-workers and are thrilled to "help out",
or
Someone in a uniform who is selling to neighbors for their charity will "get the sale" most every time.

***All Key Leaders should "lead by example" and be the first to buy the products BEFORE the official kick off*** – Often groups immediately go out and ask the public to buy before being committed enough to ask its members to buy first.

Fundraising campaign leaders are many times reluctant to ask their key leadership to buy the product first, but it is absolutely necessary in order to show that 100% of their leadership is "on board" with the program.

You will be guaranteed to have a successful sale on even a modest achievement scale if you do nothing else but implement this one simple rule… requiring your leaders and Fundraising Team Members to buy products first.

When every one of your key leaders and committee members have agreed to buy the product(s), then you can report to your general membership and community that this program is worthy of their support too since your key leaders are also 100% committed enough themselves to buy the offered fundraising products.

You never want your regular members or those in the community asking one of the leaders… "Did you participate or purchase an item?" and the answer be "no". You can then bet the person asked will also say no and "want to wait and see what happens" from others first, before participating themselves.

The fundraising campaign will simply not move forward, because everyone is waiting on others to be the first to shell out their money and buy one of the fundraising items.

As you approach your key leaders first, it is always wise to post a Fundraising Goal Thermometer Chart in front of them to visualize. A Fundraising Goal Thermometer Chart is very effective at getting others to see how the participation of these key leaders will help kickoff reaching the goal.

It's great for showing your key leader participation before you even kickoff your full campaign to others. This way you have already created some excitement before your Fundraising Team Members go out and gather even more supporters.

At any leadership meeting prior to your campaign kickoff, your Key Leader, Chairperson or President will ask their leadership to **Lead By Example** and be the first to buy one of the products and participate in the fundraiser.

This Key Leader signs up first and then, using a red marker, moves the goal thermometer up appropriately. He then passes out sales brochures and puts a little "peer pressure" on those present by asking them to choose one or more products and write a check for it before the close of their meeting.

Then at the end of the meeting the Key Leader will ask for the collection of brochures and orders and then pass around a red magic marker asking each individual to make their mark on the Fundraising Goal Thermometer Chart to indicate their purchase amount.

As each makes their mark, the Fundraising Goal Thermometer Chart slowly inches upwards, adding even more excitement. You can now report that the Key Leadership is totally, 100%, on board with the fundraiser.

You may even want to have a special Fundraising Goal Thermometer Chart just for your Fundraising Team Leaders and Fundraising Team Members to show their participation level. With the entire Fundraising Team committed to buying at least one item, it will show everyone else that they are also at a 100% participation level.

Do you see the magic of this? Even if nobody else in your community purchased an item, you can still claim your fundraiser was a success just because your Key Leadership and Fundraising Team participated at the 100% Participation Level.


***Adhere to a strict campaign timeline*** – This means that you set a solid Turn-In-Date which everybody is aware of and will stick to.

You can announce your timeline through a "Parent's Letter", email blast, bulletin, postcards mailing, or by directly speaking with each Fundraising Team Member.

Your complete campaign should take between 4 to 8 weeks from kickoff to final delivery of products to the end consumer. It should take no more than 2-3 weeks for the actual sales efforts to be conducted.

Any more time than this will lead to money and forms being lost, loss of sales momentum and questions about product arrival tardiness by the customers.

You should receive regular updates from your team leaders and make sure every Fundraising Team Member is fully aware of your turn-in date and understand that they cannot turn their orders and payments in late. I've laid several timeline scenarios out for you in this book.

Through regular updates from your Team Leaders (sometimes called Team Captains) to your Fundraising Team Members each week you can address any concerns immediately as they occur.

Again, stick to a strict timeframe and it will create fewer problems before you place the final product order with your fundraising product supplier allowing for timely shipments.

**Here's an example of an organization that did not follow these rules of success.** A large school decided to allow a fundraising distributor to introduce a product to their supporters in hopes of raising the extra money they needed.

They decided against appointing a Chairperson and just allowed the Distributor to pass out 500 brochures to students as they left to go home from school one day. The sales brochure given also had an accompanying "parents letter" which purportedly introduced and explained why the fundraiser was being performed.

The Principal saw no problem with initiating this fundraiser, since they were short on the funds needed for the year and was further reluctant to ask volunteers or teachers to conduct yet another fundraising effort.

The distributor was new at the job, eager and was pressured to handle everything and make it work. So the thought by the Principal was, "if it doesn't work out, then we've not lost anything, because we didn't invest any time, money or energy in allowing it to be offered." What could it hurt to try it?

After two weeks, no sales occurred. Why? Well, the school had nothing vested in the outcome. They were not on the hook for anything... no investment... no time expended... no clear goal... no volunteer manpower output... nothing. So, if it worked, fine. If it didn't work, fine.

Of course, there is a lesson in all of this. What was the problem? Well, the school did not "**take possession**" of the fundraiser... meaning, it just wasn't that important to them.

If the school had actually "taken possession" of this as a main fundraiser (or at least a significant fundraiser)... meaning it was very important to them, then it would have probably been a success depending on the right product(s) being offered and the right Chairperson in charge.

Really, the first step of taking possession by the school should have been to appoint a Chairperson from within (teacher or parent) to lead the charge and "**make it happen**".

By having the right Chairperson, there would also be proper incentives in place to drive excitement as well. The Distributor just can't do as effective of a job as one of the known key volunteer members from within the school.

The Principal should have never agreed to send sales brochures home and hope that sales would simply occur without having a **firm fundraising goal** and with enough volunteers in place to achieve it.

As it was, nobody knew how they could actually help the school financially or what the money was being raised for. Not parents. Not supporters.

Of course, I believe the main rule of success would have been for all "key leaders" in the school to buy the products first and "**lead by example**". This would be the Home Room Parents, Classroom Teachers, Principal, and Parents/Teachers… all Key Leaders.

If this success principal alone had been implemented, then there would at least have been some sales to show for the effort; thereby, creating a nominal level of success.

Obviously, there was no turn-in-date noted, which indicated that there was no **strict campaign timeline** involved. Nobody knew how long the fundraising selling period was to last; thus, many may have been waiting on their next paycheck or the one after that before deciding to purchase.

In other words, the rules of success were all avoided in this true worst-case scenario. Don't let that happen to your organization.

It should be agreed on from the start that these rules of success must be in place before beginning a fundraising campaign. This is especially important if you want to achieve real success that everybody can see.

So now that you know exactly what to do in order to achieve success and what not to do, I would like to lead you on to discussing how to select the perfect fundraising product for your organization. First, let's discover your "area of influence".

# Your Area Of Influence

Your area of influence whether local, regional, or national is of great importance as you create a successful fundraising effort. This book is focused on localized nonprofit organizations and not necessarily those of national dominance.

The reason is that coordination of manpower needed for a national campaign effort and the complexity of getting the campaign completed in a timely manner requires a full time paid staff member for large efforts like those with national organizations.

As you'll see, online technology seen in the **Future Trends** section of this book is best designed for large scale fundraising which national organizations must have to be successful.

Most people reading this book are looking for helpful information, because they have not started a fundraiser before. Perhaps that applies to you. More than likely you are doing this as a volunteer and your time is limited.

It takes time to recruit and train Fundraising Team Members or participants. It's not hard, but the more people you have involved, the more logistics it will require which may be beyond the scope and time you have available.

I remember organizing a Popcorn Fundraiser through my large Scout District I served at. The area of influence was a small regional effort involving several cities in the county.

There were over 70 different Units made up of Cub Packs and Scout Troops involved. We had Popcorn Colonels (kind of a play on words that's what we called the Chairperson) for every unit involved. We had to have training similar to what is highlighted in this book. There were available product flyers, sales forms, money envelopes, campaign instructions and more.

So, you must look at the size of your area you will be targeting. If it is your home town or city then proceed with the instructions in this book. If there are more than 4 counties or parishes involved, then you should make sure you choose a Chair for each to break it down into sub-groups or sub-campaigns and duplicate these instructions for each.

Keep the area of influence in mind as you begin to set up your campaign, because it will determine the complexity and how far out geographically you will need to go from your community home base.

It will also clue you in on how many Fundraising Team Members you will need as you secure the proper amount of campaign leaders to handle it all.

# Securing Your Fundraising Campaign Leadership

Before I get into the details of how to secure the proper campaign leadership, it should be understood that promoting your Product Fundraiser in a consistent manner will provide the greatest impact for your income potential.

Obviously, you'll need some help being consistent and that's why you'll need to recruit the proper fundraising campaign leadership to do so. This may possibly mean even recruiting a Fundraising Committee to set your fundraising efforts in motion.

There are 3 general emphases directed by any leadership effort ensuring the success of your product fundraiser and it all boils down to telling others.

1. <u>First, your leadership should educate your group members</u> before going to the community. At the earliest convenient time, your members should be made aware of your organization's Product Fundraising Campaign. Members definitely want to help their own organization, but need to be made aware of the products available for purchase and how they can become a Fundraising Team Member and offer these products to others. When you ask your membership to volunteer, you must get them to understand the time commitment you are expecting from them. Will they be helping for 2 weeks, 6 weeks, 3 months or a year?

2. <u>Next, your members and supporters have to be asked to do something specific.</u> You've got to invite them to actually participate in YOUR Product Fundraising Campaign - to help approach supporters - to encourage others to buy - to help promote your fundraising effort in general. You will want them to understand how important their own buying decision translates into actual income for your organization and cause.

3. <u>Finally, your ever expanding list of new supporters may want to share your product fundraiser with others.</u> Asking for referrals is something we all do. So, every member and supporter should be encouraged to promote your fundraiser and offer "word-of-mouth" advertising to help out.

The discussion below breaks these emphases in more manageable details. Let's start with setting up the infrastructure for your fundraising efforts.

As you tell others, you might need a Fundraising Committee to support your efforts unless you already have one. If your organization is small, you may want to skip this process. Usually, if you have only two to three dozen members, creating a Fundraising Committee may be too cumbersome.

For smaller groups, simply having a Fundraising Chair or Campaign Chair would work best instead of creating a whole committee. This individual can then recruit helpers as needed.

For those larger groups of 50 or more members, you may want to establish a firm foundation for your fundraiser first by creating a Fundraising Committee.

Remember, the only reason you need a Fundraising Committee is to help spread the work load. The worst thing you can do is to place one person in charge for implementing any fundraising program without any help offered.


The Fundraising Committee

Early on you will want to form or have a Fundraising Committee in place. This committee will be instrumental in implementing your organization's long term fundraising plans.

Recruiting your Fundraising Committee should be done by the top two leaders in your organization. For instance, it should be the Chair and Co-Chair, Pastor and Chairman of The Deacons, President and Vice President or similar.

1. The CEO should make a list of potential Fundraising Committee Members. Perhaps 12 people should be placed on the list at first and ranked by preference. They should be real "go getters" and able to make a big donation themselves when necessary. Do NOT ask individuals who have never given to your organization or have only given minor amounts of money to your group. They may be good tireless workers, but really don't belong on your Fundraising Committee if they are not committed and dominant givers. The

Fundraising Committee Member should be the type of individual who has the potential to give sizeable gifts. This person should hold a high level of respect in the community and can get big projects accomplished by involving others. <u>This person should not feel uneasy about asking people to help or give.</u>

2. The CEO should call the first choice on the list and make an appointment. Then proceed through the list as the individuals are either recruited or decline. You may decide to recruit your Fundraising Committee Chair first as your most prominent selection and then get that person on board before recruiting other members. There is a Job Description at the end of this book for the Fundraising Committee Chair.

3. At the meeting with the potential recruit, with assistance from your Vice-CEO, be clear about what you are asking the person to do.

4. Review with them the Job Description sheet for the Fundraising Committee Member position which is posted at the end of this book. Feel free to adapt any of the Job Descriptions in a way to suit your particular group.

5. Show this fundraising book to them and explain that it will help cut their learning curve considerably. Better yet, buy them their own copy of the book and present it to them.

6. Get a clear commitment to hold the position for at least a year.

7. The CEO and Fundraising Committee Chair then work on recruiting the rest of the Fundraising Committee.

If you already have a Fundraising Committee, then simply proceed to the next step of Securing Your Fundraising Campaign Chair. It shows how to recruit the top person who will be responsible for the Product Fundraising Campaign.

The Real Value Of A Fundraising Committee

Securing some assistance for your Fundraising Campaign Chair should be your first goal. Simply put, the Fundraising Campaign Chair cannot do this fundraiser alone and should not be expected to "go it alone".

This is where your Fundraising Committee becomes invaluable. Without a Fundraising Committee to support the Fundraising Campaign Chair's efforts, you will fall far short of achieving a successful fundraising emphasis for your nonprofit group.

Getting other people involved helps share the work load. It makes for more efficiency and opens up new possibilities through sharing of ideas and tasks.

Additionally, as Fundraising Committee Members become a customer first, they will set the pace as leaders of your fundraising efforts. They are now "leading by example" as the regular membership examines the need for their own participation.

These leaders now have a vested interest in helping ensure the success of the fundraiser and will be happy to assist the Fundraising Campaign Chair reach the funding goals.

## Securing Your Fundraising Campaign Chair

Now, let's move on to getting help with your Product Fundraising Program.

If you are reading this book and you are the President, CEO, Executive Director, Principal, Chairperson, Pastor or Minister, basically the head of your organization, you should quickly secure a Campaign Chair to steer all efforts for your fundraising campaign.

If you have a Fundraising Committee Chairperson, then work with that person to recruit someone from within your Fundraising Committee who will only handle this particular Product Fundraising Campaign. This person should not be holding down multiple volunteer jobs or positions. They must be able to totally focus on this one program and take possession to make it successful.

Let's discuss how to recruit your Campaign Chair. You will find a Job Description sheet at the end of the book. Incidentally, this technique is very similar to how to recruit Fundraising Committee Members.

1. Meet with your prospective Campaign Chair and be clear about what you are asking the person to do.
2. Review with them the Job Description sheet for the **Fundraising Campaign Chair** position (posted at the end of this book).

3. Highlight this Product Fundraising Book and explain that it will help cut their learning curve considerably. Give them their own copy for a reference.
4. Show any product flyers or brochures of past fundraisers and those being considered. If this is the first fundraising attempt, you should share with them what product interests are being considered and get their input.
5. Get a clear commitment to hold the position for as long as the campaign is active or up to a full year to help with transitioning a new Fundraising Campaign Chair to run it next time.
6. Mention that they should lead by example and be one of the first people to participate and buy a product.

There are more extensive discussions later in the book about setting up the proper campaign leadership structure depending on the size of your fundraising effort.

# Selecting Your Product

Now that we've discussed setting up the Campaign Leadership we need to shift our attention to selecting your product. You have two routes to take as you select the right product for your fundraiser:

1. Make your own products – have items that are custom made elsewhere or secure products locally and then sell at a profit.

2. Select products already made - work with a professional Fundraising Distributor who represents one or more national product company lines, sell the products you select from them and then make a profit.

In this book I'll be discussing option number two, because it is the simplest route to take for now.

Basically, by working with a fundraising professional you need only select the kind of item you want to sell and then... (a) secure enough brochures for your team to highlight the chosen fundraising product or... (b) secure your fundraising items for an on-the-spot sales campaign.

Ask your fundraising distributor or supplier if there is a possibility to personalize your product with your organization's name and logo on the label. This works great for pizza cards, sandwich cards, novelty snacks, special sauces, or other items where printing and/or a custom label is available.

Here are some key questions which you'll need to ask yourself as you consider your fundraising product campaign.

- ➢ When will your organization want to conduct the fundraiser?
- ➢ How much does your organization need to raise?
- ➢ How much time will your organization require before you need the funds?
- ➢ What product(s) would your organization want to offer?
- ➢ Is there a market for your product with your target consumer?
- ➢ Is there a unique value to your products recognizable by the consumer?
- ➢ Will it be easier to offer an "On-The-Spot" Fundraiser, Online Website Sales Campaign or order taking Brochure Sale Fundraiser?
- ➢ Will you offer products with "Home Delivery" or the customary "Delivery By Seller" method?
- ➢ Will you offer an extra "tag" product item to compliment your main fundraising product selection?

Let's look a little more closely at these questions.

<u>When will your organization want to conduct the fundraiser?</u>

Selecting the proper time of the year to conduct your fundraiser will mean the difference between success or a complete flop.

Fall is by far the favorite season for fundraising. In fact, roughly 60% - 70% of product fundraisers are conducted from late August through Mid-December.

Fall is the time when most people tend to support high school sports teams, form new scout groups, see cheer groups begin their new school year, clubs recruit students and start a new season of activity, and many nonprofits begin to conclude their year-end fundraising goals.

So you can see why so much fundraising activity and volunteer effort occurs during the fall. You will also find that about Mid-December through February 1st, fundraising activity is virtually nonexistent.

People typically don't want to be bothered during the holiday season with fundraising and they tend to not think about starting their Spring Fundraising Season until after January has passed.

During the Spring, everyone rushes to make the final push to raise enough money for the last of their projects which need funding. The Spring Fundraising Season generally begins the first part of February and extends through Mid-May.

As you may expect, around the first of May, parents and groups begin to wind down their school year projects in anticipation for summer activities. Actually, during most of the summer, through early August, not much fundraising activity occurs at all except for planning and recruiting of the fundraising team members.

There are always exceptions to these rules. For instance, some youth groups will hold large yard sales and car washes during the summer months. Many sports teams and summer mission trips may still need to raise funds, while church youth groups, band and cheer groups will raise money for Summer Camps during late Spring.

You will want to maximize the times of the year which you can secure volunteers; as well as, draw interest from supporters when they would expect to be called upon.

"Non-product fundraisers" like car washes, lend themselves to outdoor type projects involving lots of manpower when the weather is conducive and dominate the summer over product fundraising sales.

Therefore, choose a time for your fundraising campaign when you can recruit available volunteers and when you can reach the largest number of potential buyers. I tend to think of October as the ideal month to conduct product fundraising sales.


How much does your organization need to raise?

Besides the obvious question of "how much does your organization NEED to raise", you must also take into account the "amount of money your group is ABLE to raise"?

The ability to raise the money you need must answer several questions. This will ultimately help analyze the product you finally end up choosing, like:

1.) How many volunteers will you have helping you? – Small (1 dozen or less), Medium (several dozens), Large (100+ Fundraising Team Members).

2.) What is the relative size of the funds needed? – Large (over $3,000), Medium ($1,000 - $3,000), Small (under $1,000).

3.) What is the percentage of profits you are offered per item? – 40%, 50%, 90%.

Let's take a look at a few scenarios to analyze further; starting with how many volunteers you will have at your disposal.

**Small Group Scenario #1** - If you have a small group of 8 members which needs to raise a small amount of money, say $800, then you can easily choose a candy bar fundraiser as ideal. At the time of this writing, chocolate bars still sell for $1 each retail and groups usually make 50 cents per bar. That would be about $100 of profits to be raised per person. It would necessitate selling 200 bars each which would typically be one case per person (50 bars per carrier – 4 carriers per case).

**Small Group Scenario #2** - If you are a small student club of 10 which needs to raise a medium amount of funds, perhaps $2,000 for a trip, then you will have to choose a higher dollar profit per item. Let's go with candles which sell for $10 each where the club earns a 50% profit or $5 per candle sold. This would necessitate selling 400 candles or 40 candles per student. That's a stretch, but it is doable for a committed club.

**Medium Group Scenario** – If a Medium Size association of 50 members needs to raise $3,000 for a local park playground, then it should look for an even higher profitable product line like cookie dough. Cookie dough selling for $14 each tub where the association earns 45% profit or $6.30 per tub sold would necessitate selling 476 tubs or roughly 10 cookie dough tubs per member (10 tubs X $6.30 = $63 profit each member makes).

**Large Group Scenario** - Let's imagine a high school band has 100 members and they have three main functions to raise money for: 1. Uniform expenses at $50 per student, 2. Trip to play at a college football bowl performance including transportation and lodging at $150 per student, 3. End of the year trip to a theme park, including transportation and lodging, at $100 per student. This comes to a total of $300 per student or $30,000 as your starting goal. Now add a 10% contingency, if you like, for a final goal of $33,000.

Take that $33,000 and quickly eliminate low profit products like candy and treats. As we've already discussed, chocolate bars will only bring in a maximum of 50 cents profit for each one sold. Candy bars sold for $1 each would simply take too long to reach the goal. It would take much more effort than if you were selling cookie dough or candles.

The band leadership decides on Discount Merchant Cards which sell for $10 each where the band earns 100% (90% profit plus extra free cards adds a 10% bonus for purchased volume = 100%) per card sold. This would necessitate selling 3,300 cards or 33 cards per student.

You now see that you must take all of these factors into focus to determine how much money you can raise. I think you will agree that a 15 member club simply can't raise $20,000 practically without having several high-dollar generating fundraising products, as well as, conducting campaigns which are spread out over the year.

Try to avoid extremely high individual goals for your team members to reach. In the end you must also consider establishing a goal which is both attainable by each member and profitable for the group.

How much time will your organization require before you need the funds?

Will you need to raise funds quickly within 2 to 4 weeks or will you have several months (even up to a year) to plan and implement your fundraising campaign?

You will have to consider shipping time, processing time for custom made items and distribution time by your Fundraising Team Members to your supporters.

There are three types of fundraising timeframes to consider:

- Instant, "On-The-Spot" fundraisers – This type is moderately fast to conduct, with a week to have products shipped to you and another week to conduct the sale. Then it's finished.

- Brochure or Catalog Sales – It takes roughly two to three months to initiate and complete your fundraising campaign. You can see that this type takes the longest to conduct (but probably has the biggest payback).

- Online Website Sales – This provides an almost instant fundraising campaign with implementation and kickoff within one to several days. Plus, a website can stay active all year long and allow you to conduct subsequent fundraising campaigns with little notice needed.

Generally, Brochure Fundraisers have higher retail prices; thus, you assume you will receive more money per supporter. My feeling is if you have time to properly plan it out, the product brochure sales will bring in much higher dollar amounts than either of the other two timeframes alone.

Conversely, the On-The-Spot fundraiser and Website Sales are quick to get started, but will not necessarily bring in a lot of money. Most On-The-Spot sales involve items like candy bars or low cost treats and just don't bring a lot of money to the table, but it is a very quick method of getting some extra funds quickly.

The exception would be a Merchant Discount Card (or even scratch cards). For example, a Pizza Savings Card sold as an On-The-Spot sale for $10 each where you get up to 100% profit actually brings you $10 for each one sold. This provides a relatively quick turnaround and higher profitability.

What product(s) would your organization want to offer?

Fundraising products are as varied as the number of items found in any supermarket. The key is to select the most profitable products your membership feels comfortable promoting to the community.

For this reason, your Fundraising Committee may want to conduct a survey of your membership and neighbors in your community to determine their preferences.

You should realize that most supporters may not have a preference about the specific product you sell, because they are in it to help your organization. However, it's always useful to make your fundraiser as productive and successful as possible by choosing a product or combination of products that will encourage the most supporters to participate.

For use in selecting the fundraising product(s) for any group, I've included a Preferred Fundraising Product - Survey Form at the end of this book.

Below is a working list of fundraising products which have been traditionally used as fundraisers by others. This will give you a good place to start selecting a product.

I have **bolded** those that are generally popular with the public, but keep in mind that some not indicated in bold may also be seen as a "local hit" and could be very popular for your area.

For example, one community club was very effective selling pecans each fall and it was extremely popular. Their supporters anxiously awaited their popular Pecan Fundraiser each year.

I've *italicized* those fundraising products which are usually the best money makers generally for any group to offer. This doesn't mean that others not italicized will not be good money makers in your local area. It just suggests those products which typically bring in more profit per item sold.

An "O" after the name indicates it is usually an "On-The-Spot" sales product, a "B" indicates a typical "Brochure Sale" product line (may also be called pre-sale, catalog sales or flyer sales), and a "W" means that it has appeared as an Online Website Fundraiser Sales. The most prevalent will be shown first in order to the least used last.

Finally a "P" means it is a good fundraising product requiring little or no minimum orders which can be used effectively by individuals raising funds for a charity by themselves, individuals for their own personal needs, or very small groups (10 or less).

To recap:
**B** = Brochure Sales
**O** = On-The-Spot Sales
**P** = Personal, Individual or Small Group Fundraiser
**W** = Online Website Sales
**Bolded - Most Popular With Public**
*Italicized - Best Money Makers*


## Here are the most typical fundraising products being offered today:

*Auction Kits* (live, silent, balloon ride, signed sports memorabilia, etc.)  **O, W**

Back To School Supply Kits  **B**

**Baked Goods** (pies, cakes, brownies, cinnamon rolls, braided bread)  **B, O**

Ball Caps (national sports, local themed) **O, B**

Bath Products (shower gels, soaps, skin lotions, fizzes) **B**

Batteries (personal sizes for electronics, flashlights) **B, O**

Bedding and Sheet Sets **B, O**

**Beef Snacks** (jerky, links) **O**

*Beverages* - Flavored (teas, coffees, cappuccinos, cocoas, chais) **B, O, P**

**Books** (used, new, inspirational) **B, O, P, W**

*Bricks* (tiles, bricks of all sizes) **B, W**

Brittle (peanut, pecan, sugar coated nuts, crunch's) **B, O, P**

Build-A-Mascot Stuffable Toy Animal Kits **B, O**

**Bumper Stickers** / Buttons / Emblems (customized sports team, mascot) **B**

*Calendars* (personalized, local attractions or pre-designed themes) **B, O, P**

*Candles / Fragrances* (triple scented, soy, paraffin, potpourri, diffusers) **B, P**

**Candy** (tart, fizzle, gummi, fruit, licorice) **O, P**

**Candy Bars / Chocolate Bars** (national name brand, specialty brands) **O, P**

Ceramics (figurines, collectors, anniversary, Christmas ) **B**

Cheese and Cheese Spreads **B**

Cheesecakes (frozen) **B**

*Chocolate Box Assortments* (truffle, cherry, cream, cluster, turtle) **B, P**

**Chocolate Treats** (coconut, coated nuts, malted milk balls, mints) **B, P**

Chocolate Lollipops (white, milk or dark chocolate flavors) **O, P**

Clothing and Accessories (sleepwear, flip-flops, sunglasses) **B, W**

*Coffee* (flavored, gourmet) **B, O, P, W**

*Coins* (commemorative, collectors) **B, O**

*Consignment Santa Gift Shops* **O**

*Cookbooks* (pre-printed by author, custom self-published by club) **B, O, P, W**

*Cookie Dough* (dry mix, frozen, fresh, eCard) **B, W**

*Coupon Books* (grocery savings, local merchants, national name brands) **O**

*Christmas Trees* (natural, flocked, imitation) **B, O**

Cups, Mugs and Glasses (sell the mug, sponsorship ads on the back) **O**

**Cupcakes** (specialty, themed related) **O**

**Custom Printed Items** (ceramic mugs, sports bottles) **O**

Dinner Entrees (frozen, Mexican wraps, meat pies, casseroles) **B**

*Discount Merchant Cards* (sub sandwich, pizza, favorite restaurant) **O, P**

Dog Tags / Spirit Tags (personalized, themes, sports) **B, O**

Dried Fruit (for trail mixes, healthy snacks – dates, bananas) **B, O, P**

Ecofriendly Cleaning Products (cleaners, soap, detergent, sanitizers) **B, O, W**

Fire Extinguishers **B, O**

*First Aid Kits / Safety Kits* (roadside flares, bandages, etc.) **B, O, P, W**

**Flags / Wind chimes** (applique nylon flags, collegiate, house and garden) **B**

*Flowers / Bulbs* **B, W**

*Fresh Fruit* (apples, oranges, pears, grapefruit, etc.) **B, O**

**Frozen Food and Desserts** (cheesecake, Stromboli, French bread pizza) **B**

**Fruit Baskets / Crates** – homegrown strawberries, peaches, apples **B, O**

Fruit Cakes **B, O, P**

Fruit Preserves/Jams/Jelly/Local Honey (personalized, national brand) **B, O, P**

**Fudge** (homestyle, premium) **B, O, P**

*Game Books* (heavily advertised) **O**

Gifts Items (holiday, birthday, Mother's Day, Father's Day) **B**

Gift Wrap (seasonal, religious, all-occasion) **B**

***Golf Sponsorship Kits*** (indoor putt-putt, hole-in-one, golf marathons, through campus soft-golf ball, glow-in-the-dark night golf, etc.)  **O**

Gourmet Food Items (dry soups, muffin/bread mixes, dips, sauces)  **B, P**

**Greeting Cards** (everyday, holiday, etc.)  **B, O, P**

Handcrafted Wood Item/Craft (spelling family names, religious saying)  **O, B, P**

**Holiday Gift Catalog** (ornaments, statues and novelties)  **B**

***Home Décor*** (Window and Wall Decorations, plaques, fragrances)  **B, P, W**

**Hot Drink Dry Mixes** (cocoa, cappuccino, herbal tea, spiced tea)  **B, O, P**

Household Items (useful to make life easier)  **B**

***Jewelry*** (fashion, designer, local specialty)  **B, O, P**

**Kettle Korn** (homemade)  **O, B**

***Kitchen Tools*** (pans, engraved bake ware, plastic containers)  **B, P**

***Knives / Cutlery*** (sets or individual knives)  **B, P**

Lapel Pins (collectors, commemorative)  **O, B**

Light Bulbs (CFL's, LED's, solar, anti-bug, garden lamps)  **O, B**

**Lollipops** (theme related, sports related, various flavored)  **O, P**

***Magazine Subscriptions*** (using catalog, gift cards, online signups)  **B, P, W**

Meat Snacks (non-jerky sausages, mustards, cheeses, condiments)  **B**

Miniatures and Replicas  **B, O**

**Mother's Day Flowers / Corsages**  **O, B**

Muffins (healthy, local or national brand)  **O, B, P**

Music CD's  **B, O**

*Office and School Supplies*  **W**

Ornaments (ceramic and metal)  **B**

***Nuts*** (almonds, peanuts, pecans, cashews)  **B, O, P**

Paintings, Picture Frames and Prints  **B**

*Peel-It Coupon Cards*  O, P

Pens (fancy, special)  **B, P**

Pet Treats / Toys  **B, O**

Phone Cards  **B, O, P**

*Pizza* (Fresh or Frozen)  **B**

*Pizza Cards* (local favorite or national chain)  **B, O, P**

**Plants and Flowers**  O, B

Plates (dinner gold rimmed - historic, commemorative, anniversary)  **B**

*Popcorn* (kettle corn, microwave, various flavors, chocolate mixed)  **B, O, P**

Posters (special events, artistic)  O, B

**Pretzels** (cinnamon, plain) and (make-it-yourself kits or frozen)  **B, P**

Quilts (handcrafted)  **B, O, P**

*Restaurant Savings Gift Card*  O, W

**Sauces** (hot, pepper, salsa)  O, B, P

**Scented Pencils and Pens**  O, P

*Scratch Cards* (for straight donations, offering prizes) and (standard or custom designed)  O, P

*Seat Cushions* (with or without advertisements)  O

Silicone Wristbands (personalized or with standard phrases)  O, P

**Snacks** (fruit rollups, energy bars, rice krispy bars)  O, P

Soap Products (soap, shampoo, oils, lotions)  **B, P**

Spices (sea salt, barbeque rubs, local favorites, flavorings, etc.)  **B, O**

Spirit Items (besides t-shirts... megaphones, clothing, signs, etc.)  O, W, P

**Sports Themed Items** (bobble-heads, pennants, cards, drink cups)  **B, O**

Stationery (list makers, custom letterhead, etc.)  **B**

Sunglasses (import and designer)  **O, B, P**

Sun Tan Lotions  **O, B**

*T-Shirts* (unique design or from numerous designs shown in catalog)  **B, W**

*Throws / Blankets* (commemorative, sports, anniversary)  **B, O**

Toys (unique wooden, novelty or in-demand items)  **B, P**

**Trail Mixes** (various recipes with nuts, candy buttons, yogurt, raisins, etc.)  **O, B, P**

Trash Bags  **B, O**

*Two Year Planners* (pocket sized – personalized or pre-designed)  **B, O, P**

Wall Plaques With Quotable Sayings  **O, P**

**Water Bottles With Water** (personalized labels)  **O**

Wild Bird Food  **O, B**

*Wreaths* (Christmas, patriotic)  **B**

**Yearbook Sales  B**


<u>Is there a market for your product with your target consumer?</u>

This is something that some people don't think about before jumping into a fundraiser.

Keep in mind it all depends on:

A. the time of year you approach consumers

B. your geographic area of influence

C. what your target consumer typically prefers to buy.

For instance, East Coast groups have done a very good job of selling colorful house flags and garden flags through brochure sales during the fall and spring time from the states of South Carolina up the East Coast, but rarely do the flags sell elsewhere in the country or during the summer months.

Perhaps you are in a mature adult living community, it is doubtful your organization could sell candy bars or candy treats, while two year planners would do quite well. Certainly chocolate bars do not sell very well during the heat or at temperatures greater than 75 degrees.

You could easily sell commemorative plates, coins or throws for a museum fundraiser or a community anniversary celebration during the summer, but would have difficulty selling wrapping paper during the summer months.

Of course candy and snacks will always do well with students or youth organizations, but it is doubtful these same youth would want to purchase spices or soap products.

It would be easy to sell fashion jewelry to women and young ladies; whereas, you will not make any headway with a crowd of boy scouts.

Selling a Pizza Discount Merchant Card (offering a buy 1 get one free deal) to a rural community of 4,000 seems like a good idea. Right? "Everybody loves pizza," you say. What if the closest pizza outlet is in a larger community of 10,000 that is 25 miles away?

So, without a local pizza storefront present, the huge 90% profit offered by the Pizza Card will not generate much money and in the end will cost you a lot of time and effort. It might also cost you bad publicity and a "soured" group of fundraising workers who will not want to do another fundraiser as one of your volunteers.

Sure, most supporters who buy a pizza card will be going to a nearby larger community to shop every now and then and will get pizza, but could they use the card enough times where they believe they'll get their money's worth? It's a stretch at best.

Selling cookie dough to adults before the Winter holidays is a snap, but would not work at all if sales were conducted during the summer months to the same group of customers.

Be wary of fundraising companies hyping products with huge Profit Percentages. For example, a restaurant savings card showing a good 50% profit or even a 100% profit, but has just one location which might be inconvenient to 80% of your community supporters and will not raise the money you would anticipate.

I think you get the picture. Find out who your target customer will be and tailor your product selection toward maximizing sales within that marketable setting.

## Is there a unique value to your products that is recognizable by the consumer?

The items you offer must have a unique value. By a "unique value", I mean that a supporter can't find a similar item sold by a local merchant at a lesser price. The value must also be reasonable and not appear to be "overpriced."

Consumers may pay a little bit over the customary price if it is helping a worthy cause, but you can't expect them to pay two to three times what an item is normally worth.

Value of anything has hidden personal preferences, but everybody has an idea of what a name brand chocolate bar costs at the convenience store. If you try to sell it for an extra 50 cents above what can be obtained at a store, don't count on being as successful as if you were offering a specialty chocolate bar which can't be found in stores.

The consumer has nothing to compare the generic chocolate bar to at a store, so they have to make a "value decision" which might be difficult. Barring that, they will most likely revert to the concept of "supporting a worthy cause" and pay the dollar for the candy.

I use a good rule of thumb, acquired over the years, that 40% of people you approach will likely buy items priced under $10, another 40% will feel comfortable buying items priced between $10 and $20 and the remainder will buy items priced $20 or more, but not over $30. It's pretty simple really.

Now, this may change depending on the financial climate or area you are selling in.

Therefore, the income level of the marketable consumers you'll be approaching will need to be considered.

Selling $10 boxed chocolate treats will certainly not be feasible for Junior High Students to even consider selling to their peers.

47

If you approach a low-income community and offer organic cookie dough at $15 per tub, you will not be making too many sales if any.

What about niche product categories? I remember awhile back when some nonprofit groups used one of the "ecofriendly" products just coming out. They were CFL light bulbs and heavy duty trash bags. Both offered useful consumable items, but weren't well received by the public. They were perceived to be over priced from what the consumers believed they could get at the supermarket.

For instance, just as soon as the CFL light bulb fundraiser came out on the market, a large national retailer came out with very similar bulbs at three for the same price as the one bulb offered with the fundraiser.

What does a CFL light bulb mean to the consumer of one brand over the other? Not much. Probably the same as choosing one incandescent light bulb brand over another. The cheapest one is often thought to be just as useful as the higher priced one.

Now the trash bag fundraiser did offer heavier and thicker bags than what could be purchased at the store, but the prices were about 75% higher than the thinner versions available.

It's hard to measure the value of the two types of bags until you actually get a chance to use them both. So the only comparison buyers had to go on was "price".

What if the consumer liked the heavy duty trash bags? How could they get more? They didn't want the hassle of trying to run down the person who sold them the bags.

So you see, your supporters may only want unique items available which they can't get locally or at a similar price if another brand is offered.

Will it be easier to offer an "On-The-Spot" Fundraiser, Online Website Sales Campaign or order taking Brochure Sale Fundraiser?

Generally, there are three distinct methods to offer fundraising products to supporters:

- Brochure Sales

- On-The-Spot Sales

- Online Website Sales

**Brochure Sales** – A Brochure Sale Fundraiser is where the seller (Fundraising Team Member) uses an order taking form along with a colorful sales flyer, catalog or brochure and shows it to a potential supporter (customer) face-to-face where the customer chooses one or more products from the brochure, pays for their items upfront and has the product delivered to them later. The nonprofit group places a bulk order and once received, has the items distributed by their team members to the customer.

This type of fundraiser can also be referred to as a Pre-Sale Fundraiser or Order Taker Fundraiser.

The advantages of a Brochure Sale Fundraiser are that...

1. The colorful sales flyer or brochure will do much of the telling and selling for the fundraising worker, so they don't have to explain items.

2. There is typically much more variety than the other two methods; thereby, increasing the likelihood of a sale with at least one product catching the eye of the supporter.

3. A wide range of prices are offered. Higher prices will give you the highest possible profit potential while at the same time lower prices can be offered to those supporters with a limited budget who still wish to help support the cause.

4. Collecting your funds at the point-of-sale still allows your group to access its profits as quickly as possible. I advise groups to never... and I mean never... offer a "cash on delivery" basis. There are many reasons why I advise to only take payment at the time of the sale and not later when you deliver the product. There are just too many unnecessary hassles with C.O.D. which you don't need to take on.

5. The organization always orders the exact number of items needed, because they were told exactly what was needed as supporters

selected their products.  There is never a problem being stuck with extra items which do not sell.


**On-The-Spot Sales** – On-The-Spot Sale Fundraiser is where a seller (Fundraising Team Member) takes a product "in hand" (i.e. chocolate bar) and offers it for cash to a supporter (customer) face-to-face where the customer leaves with the product after the transaction is complete.

Sometimes this is called Direct Sale Product Fundraisers.


The advantages of an On-The-Spot Sale Fundraiser are that…

1. You don't have to deliver a product later to your supporter since they receive it on-the-spot.  This saves time and energy for your workers or Fundraising Team Members.

2. You also don't have to worry about damaged items or products needing to be returned since they should be in good shape at the point-of-sale.

3. It will help you have a consistent goal for each worker.  For instance, give two cases of $1 candy bars (50 bars each) per student to sell for a personal goal of $50.

4. The sales timeframe is short.  You can sell out of your products in a couple of days and can then order more to increase your profits or you can decide to end the sale.

5. Although there is less variety, it also makes for fast decision making from supporters; thus, being able to engage many more supporters who perhaps don't have the time or desire to review a brochure or go online to purchase an item.


**Online Website Sales** – The Online Website Sale Fundraiser utilizes online technology to sell, complete the transaction and even provide an instant receipt. It's like having your very own eStore packed with a bunch of items for sale as a fundraiser. Instead of seeing someone face-to-face, you can easily utilize a fast email fundraising campaign which will allow you to even reach supporters all over the country.

The best part about the online website sales program is that products are typically delivered straight to your supporter's home.

The advantages of an Online Website Sale Fundraiser are that...

1. Your group does not require as many volunteers (Fundraising Team Members) to conduct an effective fundraiser. A few individuals with lots of email contacts can potentially engage many more people.

2. Since it can reach out to people all across the country, it is not as confined to a local area like on-the-spot sales or brochure sales would necessitate. Remember, those methods require delivery of products to customers in person.

3. You can operate your fundraiser 24/7... even while you are asleep... online and by email.

4. There are no products to deliver since the products are sent from the online product company and delivered straight to the customer's home.

5. Websites are kept running all year long which can lead to additional sales. New sales can occur through occasional email reminders to customers as new items are added or a special need occurs. Simply send an email, postcard or letter out to all of your customers reminding them to go to your fundraising website for the new offer or promotion.

6. There are no money handling problems since the product company handles all transactions online and sends your funds made from the sales shortly thereafter.

Normal fundraisers could take weeks to conduct and conclude your campaign, order your products in bulk and then distribute to the proper customer when they finally become available at home. Brochure fundraisers can take weeks... perhaps as much as 8 weeks to get the selected fundraising products to customers.

That's not good for anyone. Why not show your supporters that you will take care of their support purchases quickly?

As soon as they are invited to support your efforts by going to your fundraising website (which is given to you by the fundraising company)... then buy one or more items... the items are immediately shipped out (usually within a couple of days) straight to their personal address.

Everybody is happy! Everybody wins!


OK. Now for the important question on choosing one of these three options.

How much does it cost to start?

- Typically, Online Website Sales and brochure sales of fundraising products don't cost anything to start. Websites are provided by the fundraising company at no charge.

- Sales brochures and sales order forms are provided free to the group. Usually one brochure and sales order form is sufficient for each Fundraising Team Member.

- On-The-Spot Sales do require you to pay for items upfront before they are shipped to you. Granted you will receive your profits back when you sell all of your items, but there is still an upfront cost to start.


If time becomes an issue, I suggest you consider good online website sales program. As I mentioned, the product is delivered straight to the customer's home so you avoid a lot of time taken by typical brochure sales deliveries.

Many individuals have raised money very fast through online fundraising programs by getting their friends and relatives from all over the country to support their efforts and by asking them to help reach their personal goal within a matter of days.

I advise you to carefully study how much time that you have available to conduct your fundraiser, then make your decision on the actual product and type of fundraiser that will help you with that allotted timeframe.

## Will you offer products with "Home Delivery" or the customary "Delivery By Seller" method?

A Home Delivery Fundraiser has products which can be delivered straight to the end-consumer's home! The online fundraisers almost exclusively offer delivery to the customer's home address, but some brochure sales also allow for home delivery.

Therefore, you should ask your fundraising distributor or supplier if they offer home delivery of the products. Of course, on-the-spot sales bypass this issue of deliverability entirely.

There are two unique situations where it may be advantageous to select a fundraiser where home delivery is a part of the fundraiser.

1. Your club or group is spread out across a particular region or the entire country.

2. Your group or organization is very small, but aggressive and anticipates making a lot of sales, but doesn't want to be burdened with the many hours needed to distribute products to supporters.


Of course home delivery takes the hassle out of delivering products back to your supporters which save your team members extra expenses while doing it within a matter of a few days.

Sometimes team members lose or damage items as they make their deliveries. So a home delivery option has the advantage of virtually guaranteeing delivery and arrival to the supporter much quicker, by as much as four weeks sooner than traditional product deliveries.

Get with your chosen Fundraising Company or Distributor and ask what products they offer for home delivery.

Some of the products that are ideal for home delivery include flower bulbs, cookie dough, Christmas wreaths, personalized cards and stationery, coffee, office supplies and magazines. Look for Online Fundraising Programs initially and then Home Delivery as a subheading under the Fundraising Products category on your Fundraising Company or Fundraising Distributor websites.

## Will you offer an extra "tag" product item to compliment your main fundraising product selection?

A tag item is an extra item or selection of a few items shown on a colorful sales flyer tagged onto the main product line selection usually from a larger brochure. It is an item your members believe will compliment or assist in bringing in extra profits which your main product brochure does not address or fill a need with the public.

For instance, you are selling Holiday Christmas Wrapping Paper, using a 16 page brochure highlighting various holiday designs. Then you realize that not everyone will buy wrapping paper so, you decide to add a "tag" on flyer of candles highlighting holiday scents (scents like: pumpkin spice, sugar cookie, Christmas tree, apple pie, cinnamon).

I think most customers who will need wrapping paper for the holidays might want candles as well. They could easily envision lighting their favorite holiday scented candle as they sit down to wrap gifts for their family and friends. It kind of gives you a warm, cozy feeling to know you would be inspiring their gift giving spirit.

In this case, the candle flyer tag in this case compliments the holiday wrapping paper brochure perfectly, because both are holiday oriented.

You may discover that a "tag" product could even double your profits since many customers may want at least something from each category.

# Profits To Expect

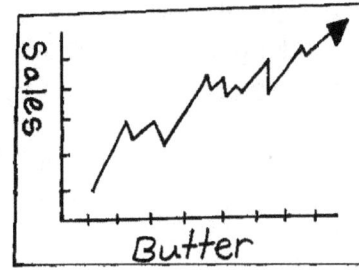

The typical fundraising product will generate for you 40% to 50% profit from its retail price. There are some products that will generate even more profits like restaurant discount cards or local merchant cards which guarantee 90% to 100% profit of the retail price.

Let's look at three important terms when dealing with profits from your fundraiser.

1. Profit Percentage
2. Actual Profit
3. Profit Potential

**Profit Percentage** – The Profit Percentage is based on the difference of what you pay to the Product Company or Fundraising Distributor for the items at wholesale (what they charge you) and what the retail value of the item is (what you charge the public).

For instance, $10 Retail Priced Item - $6 Wholesale Cost of Item = $4 Profit which would show your profit percentage as 40%.

**Actual Profit** – Now, as you may begin to realize, the profit percentage offered on a product is only half of the profit picture.

The Actual Profit would focus on the actual dollar amount that you will raise. In the above example, it would be shown as $4.00 actual profit per item sold.

The distinction should be made between the actual profit and the profit percentage, because looking at the profit percentage alone will not give you a complete profit potential picture.

The actual profit from candles at 50% profit (50% of $10 = $5) is by far greater than what you get with candy bars at the same percentage (50% of $1 = 50¢). Wouldn't you agree?

I would advise you to also check with your fundraising distributor whether the product has "levels of sales achievement" in place.

For instance, if the product has a profit percentage offered with the term "up to", then it means that you probably have sales levels to achieve in order to reach the higher profit percentages.

Let's say one fundraising company offers 45% on candles no matter how many candles you order while another company offers sales levels; whereby, only larger orders of 500 candles receive the 50% level. The latter company may only offer 35% profits for less than 100 candles ordered, 40% for 100 to 249 candles ordered, and 45% for 250 to 499 candles ordered.

If you are a small group or organization conducting several sales over the year, then it may be more advantageous to go with the company offering a consistent profit of 45% so your group is not penalized for turning in smaller size orders over the course of the year.

Of course, the reason for these sales levels has everything to do with getting a group to conduct more sales at once, because they will stretch to reach the highest profits possible. And just for the record, that's not a bad thing.

One final note about figuring actual profits. You should ask your fundraising distributor how shipping charges, custom student packing, and any offered incentives are figured into the final profit picture. I'll cover more on these later in the book.

For instance, shipping costs of cookie dough on refrigerated trucks will be a lot more expensive than having Pizza Discount Cards mailed to you. As you can see, some customary business expenses like shipping might lower your true profit potential so be sure to figure this all in your decision making.

**Profit Potential** – The Profit Potential is the way in which you should look at "profit" as you judge the fundraising products you will use in your fundraising campaign. You are ideally looking for a blending of both the Profit Percentage and the Actual Profit.

As you consider the perfect fundraising product for your organization offering the greatest profit picture, you should focus on what has the greatest Profit Potential.

Look at these products displayed below and figure out what has the greatest Profit Potential or which brings in the most money. In the chart, I will keep some variables the same so that you can focus on the profitability of the program only.

| Product | Profit % | Team Members | Items Sold Per Person | Retail Price Each Item | Actual Profit Each | Final Profit Potential |
|---------|----------|--------------|----------------------|------------------------|--------------------|------------------------|
| Candles | 40% | 100 | 4 | $10 | $4 | $1,600 |
| Snacks | 50% | 100 | 4 | $6 | $3 | $1,200 |
| Chocolate Bar | 50% | 100 | 4 | $1 | 50¢ | $200 |
| Sandwich Card | 100% | 100 | 4 | $10 | $10 | $4,000 |

You'll quickly see that even though the snacks offered a greater Profit Percentage than the candles, the final Profit Potential was less than what the candles would have generated at the lower Profit Percentage.

Finally, be sure to not look at Profit Potential as the end all of selecting a product. You should also survey your membership to see if they "will sell" the selected item.

Even though the merchant sandwich card showed the best profit potential, maybe your members would not like to sell the merchant sandwich card as much as they would the candles.

Therefore, in the end analysis, you MUST choose a fundraising product your membership will be excited about offering the public while regarding what the final Profit Potential will generate.

# Choosing Your Product Company

If you are reading this book, then you may not have the extensive knowledge of a fundraising professional. He or she will know how other groups achieved success; as well as, what did not work well for them.

Sometimes leaning on professionals with expertise in their field will pay big dividends. So, by all means, lean on the experience of fundraising professionals.

Their incentive is to make sure your organization does succeed, because it means more money in their pockets and will keep them with a solid reputation. If they are committed in reaching your goals, then they will reach theirs as well.

Not every fundraising professional needs to meet with you face-to-face. In fact, only large organizations and schools with hundreds of participants will be able to demand a local representative be on hand.

Most of the time it is just not practical or cost effective for local groups or clubs to have access to a local sales representative or distributor.

However, there are many companies which provide excellent service through their online website, social media, chat, telephone or by email. Having a professional fundraiser on hand locally who can conduct a kickoff is not necessary and might even make a group more complacent about success of their own campaign.

I've seen organizations not take leadership of their campaign seriously enough, because they were depending on someone else (fundraising – i.e. the professional) to make sure it happened for them. Remember, when I discussed earlier the success principle that YOU must "take possession" of your fundraiser and "make it happen"?

Anybody working outside of your organization, like a professional, is much more limited in what they can make happen than those within an organization who take ownership of their campaign and who can bring the necessary resources to which will ultimately lead to success.

Here are some guidelines to use when choosing your fundraising distributor or fundraising product supplier company.

Many of these answers will probably appear on the fundraising company's website, literature mailed to you, or in an email sent to you and will be discussed in more detail in certain sections of this book.

<u>What you ask your fundraising company representative or distributor</u>

1. **Introduce yourself over the telephone and ask to speak with a sales representative.** Get to know a little bit about their fundraising company and how long they've been in business. Do they belong to any professional memberships like AFRDS (Association of Fund Raising Distributors and Suppliers), Chamber Of Commerce or Better Business Bureau? Members of AFRDS are seen as reputable since membership in the organization is fairly well internally regulated. Is the distributor a member of the AFRDS and for how long? Look for the AFRDS logo displayed on their website. Not all fundraising distributors, suppliers or professionals are members of AFRDS, but they may still be a legitimate fundraising company. Just do your homework. You may even ask for references from other groups they've served or ask around your community. You may also wish to fill out an online request form asking for more information and they will mail it, email it, or call you and assist you when it's convenient for you.

2. **Ask about the specific product** you will be using and whether it is currently available. If so, request the number of brochures or flyers you will be using to offer the product (or group of products). There typically is not a cost for sales brochures to be sent to you, but you should be certain about that fact before beginning. Printing of your group's name on the brochures or flyers is rare, but may be available so you may want to ask about this service. Will the distributor supply you with Money Collection Envelopes and Guidelines on how to work the fundraiser? Do they offer a prize program with an accompanying prize sheet for each Fundraising Team Member? Are the actual sales forms printed on the sales brochure or flyer you'll be using or will the distributor be supplying the order forms separately? Will triplicate sales order forms be necessary for processing the order in the end?

3. **Are there any minimums** which you must purchase? Can you order just one item or do you have to order a certain minimum or case? Are

items shipped "to the piece" or "by the case" and if so, how many items are in a case? Can a subsequent order be placed for just a few items if you have some late order turn-ins?

4. **Ask about payment arrangements.** What forms of payment do they accept for your product order? Do they accept credit cards and if so, which ones. What about debit cards, personal checks, money orders, cashier's check, PayPal? What name should your payment check be made payable to? Is there a deposit required? Deposits are extremely rare. I personally would steer away from any company that requires any deposit. Does your product purchase require paying for the items upfront like candy bars or after a brochure fundraising campaign is completed? On-The-Spot sales items like candy bars require you to pay for the items before they are shipped to you. Note: Purchase Orders with a Net 30 payment availability is usually extended only to schools and school systems; but not to school clubs, extracurricular school groups or any other non-school organization for that matter.

5. **Ask about your profit margins.** What are your profit margins? How are your profit margins calculated? Ask whether there are any sales bonuses for achieving certain sales levels. For example, the ABC Nonprofit organization orders 10 items and are given a 35% profit. Later they order 100 items and are given a 40% profit. Much later they order 1,000 items and receive the highest profit available at 50% because they've crossed a sales threshold each time. Are you required to send in the total retail monies and are then sent a profit check back or do you keep your profits upfront and simply pay for the wholesale pricing before it is shipped? *See more on profit margins in the section **Profits To Expect** in this book.*

6. **Ask about sales taxes.** Do they require sales taxes at the time of the order? See the section on *Sales Taxes* in this book for more on the subject.

7. **Does the company offer "student packing"?** Student packing occurs when each Fundraising Team Member's order is tallied, packed and boxed specifically labeled for that team member. If so, how much does it cost? *See the section in this book on **Student Packing** for more information on this subject.*

8. **Ask about shipping and handling arrangements.** Are there any shipping costs or is the shipping free? Sometimes you receive free shipping when a certain level of sales has been achieved. What is that sales threshold? What about fuel surcharges? Can orders be shipped to the end-consumer or only to one location in a bulk order?

9. **Ask about typical delivery times** and how long the product typically takes to arrive after the final payment is made? Is it one week, two or some other timeframe? If shipping goods like chocolate, which could melt in temperatures above 75 degrees, make sure you will be shipping in weather that will keep your items from melting while in transit.

10. **Can you return items for a refund?** Some companies with specialty items like "scratch cards" which require you to buy them upfront, will let you return any unsold, non-personalized, undamaged items for a refund. You should never expect to have any food items, which you may have overbought and can't sell, be returned for any refund. This is due to food safety issues where possible contamination may occur from a Fundraising Team Member or the end-consumer, whether accidental or purposeful. In other words, the company cannot restock food items and sell to others for fear of food contamination. So, if you buy food products upfront, make sure you can sell every item and not be left with food products you can't sell in a reasonable amount of time.

11. **What is their Product Replacement Policy?** Damaged goods, missing or broken items should be easily replaced by your fundraising company, but you should still ask what kind of replacement criteria they require. Most companies place a "damage claim" with the shipping company (like UPS or FedEx) they used if the damage occurred in transit. You may be required to keep the broken items until a representative from the shipper can come by, inspect the damage and pick it up. If you have any missing items or wrong items sent, get back with your distributor as quickly as possible to correct the error. Most reputable companies will get the replacement items shipped out as quickly as possible.

12. **How does the fundraising company handle back orders or substitutions?** You can sometimes experience some manner of back orders if your organization is using a specialty sales catalog (with

various gifts and items) and are placing your order at the very end of the sales season for that catalog. For instance, there will invariably be some shortages which could occur when you place an order in Mid-December using a Winter Holidays catalog.

13. **Is there a contract?** Contracts are extremely rare. If so, I would tend to look to a company that does not require any legal paperwork in order to start your fundraiser. However, it is perfectly legitimate for fundraising companies to lend equipment, sales banners or goods on consignment and also ask you to sign a document insuring that they will be paid for their equipment which is not returned or is damaged.

14. **What other types of support will you receive?** Will there be a company representative locally who will assist you? Do they have a credible web presence? Is there an email or phone number you can call and speak with a customer service person to place your final order with? Or is there a company sales representative you can speak with if you have a problem?

These are all questions you may have for your fundraising representative or distributor. Now let's look at questions which they may have for you and your organization.

Here's what a fundraising company or distributor will need to know from you

- ➢ What product or combination of products is your group interested in offering the public?
- ➢ What is your fundraising goal?
- ➢ In your estimation, will it take more than one product fundraising campaign to reach your annual goal? Will your group be open to selling again later in the year in order to reach the final goal?
- ➢ Is the Fundraising Campaign Chair experienced or is this person new and untrained?
- ➢ How many Fundraising Team Members will you have participating?
- ➢ What is the age of your participants or who is the typical targeted purchaser?
- ➢ What fundraising products has your organization offered in the past and how successful were they?
- ➢ When do you want to conduct your sales campaign?

> What incentives, if any, have you thought about offering in order to boost sales participation and volume?

Print this list off and have the answers handy as you discuss your product fundraising campaign or email it ahead of time and wait for a timely response.

As you visit with your fundraising distributor, don't become over-bearing about "product quality". Remember, your primary goal is to raise funds and it's not, contrary to popular belief by some, to sell the best product imaginable.

Of course you never want to provide a terrible product to your supporters, but I've known of some group leaders who were so afraid of being embarrassed in some way that they insisted on having "THE perfect product with unmatched quality". They entirely overlooked what they were ultimately trying to accomplish. Which is… to raise money for their group!

My advice would be to stay focused on the primary goal of raising funds. Stay focused on raising the money you need and not so much on providing the perfect product selection for your supporters.

Once you get supporters to start thinking about "quality issues", "shopping around" and "pricing issues", then they are less apt to support your cause at their full potential.

After all, they reason, "I can get a similar cookie dough at the grocery store for a lot cheaper price, so I'll just pass for now. Thanks for stopping by."

In the end, you want your supporters to feel good about participating and supporting your fundraiser and that the money they give you for the product you're offering will be put to good use in helping you accomplish your goals.

# The Easy Art Of Asking

Asking others to give to your cause and then getting them to say "yes" to what you're requesting is extremely rewarding. There is a remarkable feeling that occurs when you truly believe in your efforts while asking other people to join with you.

The art of asking is the key to many areas of life. Children learn early on how to ask their parents for something they desire.

I remember how my oldest daughter Cindy worked magic on me by the way she asked for something she really wanted. She would start off in a very icky sweet voice, "Dad, dear Dad..." and would proceed to ask in a very sweet, polite manner which I was helpless to resist.

However, not everybody has to put the charm on someone to get the "sale". Here is a list of Success Points you'll need to perfect as you approach anybody asking them to consider your request.

> ➢ Look the person in the eye as you ask (this lets them know you want their undivided attention). Looking down or around as you ask shows you are not having a mutual conversation, rather you are lecturing or "talking down to" that person.

> ➢ Be direct and clear when speaking. In other words, don't talk to yourself or hurry through your presentation.

- Smile as you ask (a bright smile knocks down resistant barriers). Even if you are speaking with someone over the phone, you should physically smile while speaking, because it actually does come across in your conversation. People can readily sense your smile as you visit with them by telephone.

- Hand something to your potential customer as you make your request to them. When someone receives something from another person it breaks down the personal barrier and they become more inclined to review what you have to show them. This could be a brochure, sales page or picture of what you are raising money for. I often handed, to a potential donor, a small index card with the specific dollar amount written on the card of what I wanted the donor to consider. I would then point with my finger to the requested amount typed on the card (directing their attention there) and simply asked, "Would you consider helping us with this much?" There was usually a fairly quick response given whether it was a "yes" or "no".

- Thank the person often through the conversation when appropriate without going overboard. A simple 'thank you' goes a long way to let your supporter know that you value their time and generosity.

- Practice on those you know best in order to become more relaxed and conversational with others (ask parents, grandparents, relatives, co-workers, peers and neighbors first… they will easily overlook nervousness or shyness).

In the Holy Scriptures, Jesus told his disciples to "*Ask, and it shall be given you;…*" (Matthew 7:7-8) and to "*For everyone who asks receives,…*". The meaning is clear, you don't have to be spiritual or an expert salesperson to ask for what you desire.

You just need to approach someone and state your case "asking" for their assistance.

Be sure to be bold and ask like you mean it. Make sure they know you really need their help in reaching your fundraising goal.

Preparations For Asking

Certain preparations should be made before beginning to ask supporters for their help or to open up their wallets to buy one of your fundraising products.

Groups should:

❖ Set a goal and state the goal to everyone. Post a "Goal Thermometer" chart (see the **Tools And Forms** section of this book) at prominent areas where people will pass through. Hand out extra Goal Thermometers to every Fundraising Team Member to display or show supporters.

Actually ask for everyone you meet to help you reach your goal; thus, pulling people into a "partnership" role of helping your group to achieve the goal and ensure success.

While you're at it, give your campaign a special name. For instance, two examples are "WHS Band Trip To Washington DC Campaign" or "Community Club's – Send A Child To Summer Camp Campaign".

❖ Make it easy to buy a product. Provide the necessary brochure or sales order forms to your Fundraising Team Members to make their job easy. Be sure to express your timeline properly to everyone involved. A Fundraising Team Member may say to the customer, "Our fundraising campaign is three weeks long and I have one more week to sell and turn in my money. The item you purchase will then take 10 business days to arrive after the Turn In Date and I'll deliver your products within a week after they arrive".

❖ Make it simple to pay. Some groups are not accepting checks anymore; rather, only cash and certain credit cards. I would suggest using PayPal, Square or a similar online company which accepts most every type of credit card. Even checks can be posted electronically.

If customers ask for a receipt, let them know that you will provide receipts upon delivery of their product or you can email them one. Again, don't complicate things for your supporters or Fundraising Team Members.

If you feel it necessary to issue a receipt at the time of the sale, then have a standard receipt document which you've created (try Microsoft Word Templates online) with contact information and a spot where the Fundraising Team Member can place the amount paid and hand it to the supporter.

❖ <u>Make regular updates to your goal thermometer</u>. As you update the progress of your goal, consider placing nearby some prominent names of people who have chosen to buy products while mentioning typical items they purchased. Use social media websites like Facebook or create a Microsite with TotalSnap.com to post this information and then spread the word to your community and customers.

People are much more likely to mimic others and purchase if they can see what others are buying. By using a sales order form, where the customer fills out the form themselves, they will see what other purchasers are buying which helps them make an easy buying decision themselves.

Individuals should:

❖ <u>As With any introduction, clearly identify the group you are working with</u> which will add credibility to your efforts. Have a badge on (first name only for adults… No names of children displayed for safety reasons) showing your group name and logo (or mascot). You may also choose to wear your organization's uniform with permission or your group's T-Shirt for identification and credibility purposes.

❖ <u>Be bold and don't allow fear to keep you from reaching out to others</u>. Just be yourself and decide to "do it". Place a sales brochure or flyer in front of a potential buyer explaining your fundraiser and ask for their support.

❖ <u>Inform your supporter of your Goal and ask for a specific purchase quantity to help reach that goal</u>. For instance, a student might phrase it like… "Aunt Sue, my personal fundraising goal this year is to sell 10 candles with our school's Candle Fundraiser. We are using the money to build a new school playground. Would you help me reach my goal by buying 2 candles?"

❖ <u>Make sure to approach people in a positive manner</u> similar to how you would like to be approached by someone. Be polite, courteous, conscious of other's time, be bold, friendly, cheerful, and thankful. Basically, follow the major points of the Scout Law.

❖ <u>Be proud of your effort and don't be ashamed to ask for someone's support by buying a fundraising product</u>. Let them know that their financial help is vital. Actually, people love to be asked to help a worthy cause and yours is certainly worthy right?

# Fundraising Tips For Beginners

Now that you are more prepared to begin asking others, you will need some tips that will help you be the most successful you can be.

I'm often asked what tips you would give those who are new to fundraising. This is fairly easy, because I was a beginner myself once. I didn't have this knowledge to help me quickly become a success though. It took years to come up with these carefully tested principles that if you follow, you will have cut your learning curve by years.

Here they are:

1.  Make an actual list of relatives, neighbors, family friends, and co-workers who you would like to ask. Remember to start by asking your parents first (even if you are an adult), then those on your list. A list will help you focus on those likely to be more willing to help you reach your goal. You can also see progress of your efforts as you place a check mark by those you've approached.

2.  Treat every supporter as a customer with the respect due them. Thank them for their time even if they say the dreaded "No thanks". Don't accept a "no-sale" as a direct rejection of you personally. A "no" usually means that they don't have the money available or they don't like the product selection.

3.  Be honest and answer any questions to the best of your ability. Don't stutter or ramble, just give the facts that you know quickly and move on to the next question. Know your products fairly well, because nothing is worse than trying to figure it out as you are selling the products.

4.  Avoid hard sales techniques. Let the customer choose how they want to participate. You should assist them in selecting the type and number of items they want to buy. Your job is to help them feel good about supporting your organization as they choose a product to purchase.

5.  Leave some basic information with your customers on a flyer about your fundraising campaign which your leaders have prepared (name of

your organization, what the funds are being raised for, date campaign and sales will end, approximate time delivery should occur, name and number of the Chairperson or adult in charge, how they can order more products, how they can refer others to your sale, how the individual can help your group further with their financial gifts). This satisfied customer can then help you by showing this information to others, especially by posting on their social media outlets.

6. Enjoy what you are doing and have fun. Salesmanship is a worthy endeavor, so you should never need to apologize to anyone as you ask for their support.

7. Try not to robotically cite a sales pitch word-for-word. Rather when introducing yourself, simply state your name, your group name, what items you are selling and what you are raising money for. Rehearse your sales pitch before going out. Conduct trial sales techniques on those you know first, like family members, so you will feel more comfortable asking strangers later.

8. Hand the sales flyer or brochure to the potential customer and allow them to review your material and sales prices. You may assume that when they choose to receive your sales brochure in their hand, they will want to buy something, so give them plenty of time to review it. Point to the "hot items" other people have purchased.

9. Accept payment at the time of the order. Never accept a promise for them to pay later the day you approach them after selecting a product. Rather, give them another time you can check back with them so they can buy when their funds are available.

10. Choose to BE successful. Visualize yourself reaching your personal sales goal quickly and then take action. Be bold.

# On-The-Spot Sales

There are several sales methods available that should be reviewed. One of the most common fundraising sales methods is the "On-The-Spot" Sale.

The On-The-Spot Sales Fundraiser is sometimes called Direct Sales, because you have the product in-hand (i.e. candy bars) and sell direct to the customer face-to-face. Having an item "in hand" as you approach others, will often work for very quick fundraising sales.

The On-The-Spot Sale is ideal for small groups, because one or two key leaders can make a decision quickly to get started without needing to go through a committee of decision makers.

The products are usually at a low retail price, so the products move quickly. Usually $1 to $2 for candy bars, but pizza savings cards (a discount merchant card) which retail at $10 each are also good direct sale products which bring in even more profits.

Any Fundraising Team Member simply shows or hands a potential supporter the fundraising product being offered and simply state "would you like to support our group by buying a _____ for $_____?"

Your organization orders enough of the product or line of products and pays the product company upfront for the items. The items are then shipped in bulk to one location and then you divide the products so that every Fundraising Team Member has enough to sell to your supporters in the community.

Let's envision that your organization needs to raise several hundred to a few thousand dollars within a couple of weeks. You decide to order chocolate bars that same day from a reputable fundraising company or distributor.

As your order is being shipped, you can then work out the details, recruit any remaining Fundraising Team Members you need and choose your kick off date and location.

Your chocolate is delivered to your door early the following week and your group immediately begins conducting your fundraising campaign. You sell out within a week and pocket the profit. It's that Easy.

The only downside to On-The-Spot Sales is the risk of over ordering and being stuck with extra product you might not be able to sell within your sales timeframe.

**Locations Where On-The-Spot Sales Work**

- Retirement Centers
- Shopping Centers
- Office Environments
- Car Dealerships
- Worship Centers
- Public Parks
- University Parking Lots
- County Fairs
- Flea Market Booths
- Craft Events
- Festival Merchant Areas
- Restaurants
- Sporting Events
- Local Business Parking Lots
- Hardware Stores

If you are a larger group or needing to raise $4,000 or more very quickly, then it is unlikely you will be able to use this method to raise funds effectively.

It becomes almost impossible to raise a large amount of funds using the On-The-Spot Sales method. That's the job for the Product Brochure Sales method.

So let's next review how you can raise larger amounts of funds using the tried-and-true method of Product Brochure Fundraising Sales.

# Using Product Brochures

A Brochure Fundraising Sale is the traditional way for any size group to raise funds using printed brochures, flyers or catalogs displaying various product or items for sale. In fact, a Brochure Fundraising Sale can also be referred to as a Product Brochure Sale, Product Flyer Fundraiser or a Catalog Fundraising Sale by some.

It is a great way for newer nonprofit groups, with little or no funds in the bank, to grab this no-risk, no-money-upfront type of fundraiser. Materials like sales flyers, catalogs, order forms and envelopes are usually provided free of charge to the group by a fundraising company or distributor.

The Brochure Fundraising Sale typically follows a longer running campaign timeline than the On-The-Spot Sales fundraiser, but is able to bring in larger amounts of funds because of it.

It is best suited for larger organizations or schools and will take more planning to implement. However, small groups and even individuals have used this method effectively.

Brochure or catalog sales are not as restrictive as On-The-Spot Sales, because they offer a wide variety of items. Practically everyone you approach can find one or more items offered at various prices from the selection which they might wish to purchase.

You should plan to offer items that will fit the budget of your target consumer. Remember, most people are comfortable spending up to $20, but about 40% of individuals asked expect to pay for items at $10 or below.

Since your Fundraising Campaign Chair will order the products after the sale is complete, your organization only receives the exact number of items needed. This keeps any group from dealing with "over ordering" issues and having extra stock on hand that was not sold like with On-The-Spot Sales.

In a nutshell, your Fundraising Campaign Chair orders 1 brochure or sales flyer per participant (Fundraising Team Member) who then each shows it to supporters in their community. The supporter buys the number of items they want by writing it down on the sales order form and pays the retail price upfront with the expectation that within a few weeks their products will be delivered to them by this same Fundraising Team Member.

You should never allow COD for orders made. Customers should always pay for their items upfront at the time of their order.

The reason? Well, let's just say it cuts down on the number of hassles you will have later on. I've seen groups offer COD which immediately puts them on the hook for the wholesale cost of those items ordered even before they get any money from the supporters.

In these COD situations, when the products are being delivered, many times the person is not at home which then necessitates making several calls to reach that person. Sometimes the person has moved or reneges on their purchase, so now you are stuck with items that new supporters may not wish to buy.

In any case, the fundraising company will certainly not offer your group the products by COD before they have been paid for. The exception is with schools which can issue a Purchase Order and pay later.

Action Guide

This Action Guide will lead most small to medium size groups through conducting a successful Brochure Fundraising Campaign.

As you'll see starting from Phase 2 below, a Brochure Fundraising Sales Campaign typically takes between 7 to 11 weeks to complete. If you are offering your own custom products, then you will also have to figure in time to manufacture or make your items as well.

For larger groups requiring Team Leaders who then recruit Fundraising Team Members, you should see the section in the book called **The Structured Fundraising Campaign For Large Groups**.

Phase 1 – Before The Campaign (1 – 6 Months)

Prior to beginning your fundraising campaign your fundraising committee or decision making board should choose your kickoff date and get it on the yearly calendar. Check around and make sure it does not conflict with other scheduled activities, festivals or major fundraisers in the community.

Obtain the approval for this fundraiser with those in authority (Principal, President, etc.) or with your key decision making board.

Set your fundraising goal and choose the products you will offer. Use the product selection chapter shown earlier in this book to narrow your product selection or choose your own products.

Then settle on the fundraising company or distributor who carries your particular product and interview them. See the section in this book about **Choosing Your Product Company** for more information on this subject.

Some nonprofit groups select several fundraising companies and have each send them a complete packet with sample brochures, fact sheets and product overview.

They then narrow their search from these and select the specific brochure they want to use along with the profit offered.

This is a relatively effective means of making the final choice of which fundraising company they'll use based on the brochure and profits which are offered specifically in the packets.

Your selected fundraising company or distributor will give you all of the fundraising steps and details needed to complete the particular product fundraiser you've chosen.

Determine from them which product brochure you will be using and ask for samples if available.

Finally, you may want to consider adding any other Sales Flyers or small Brochures as a "Brochure Tag" to the main fundraising product brochure you'll use.

For instance, if your group is using a Candle Brochure as the main product, your Fundraising Team Members could also offer at the same time a Two Year Planner sales flyer which easily compliments the candles. Nothing could be simpler than that.

With a "brochure tag" added, the customer now has a choice of either candles or two year planners. And if they choose both, you've just increased your profits over what you would have made by only selling the candles.

Phase 2 – Team Recruitment (2-3 Weeks Before Kickoff)

Team Recruitment and preparation for the campaign usually takes 1-2 weeks to accomplish. You will need one Team Leader for every 5 Team Members you recruit. The exception to this rule would be when a teacher or Homeroom Parent can handle 20 – 30 students of each class.

Remember to use social media outlets like Facebook as an effective tool to recruit volunteer Fundraising Team Members.

Once your Fundraising Team Members are recruited, call your fundraising company or distributor and order enough of your selected flyer or brochure to secure at least one for each Fundraising Team Member. Keep in mind it takes 2-5 days for the distributor to process and ship your materials.

Be prepared for other groups to be ahead of you in the queue, so you shouldn't expect to have these items overnighted to you the next day when you call at 4pm.

Besides your actual sales Fundraising Team Members, you may want to select a support committee made up of a Publicity Chair, two to six Collectors (money counters), Accounting Manager, and a Delivery And Distribution Chair.

It's been known for packages with sales materials to be delivered by the shipper to the wrong address or even lost. You should give yourself plenty of time to have received the items and prepare them for the kickoff date.

Gather any materials you will need to use in Fundraising Team Member packets such as calendar timeline, procedures for collecting money, prize and incentives to achieve, introductory or parent's letter.

Train your Fundraising Team by having an official Kickoff at a certain physical location and time or simply have your Team Leaders make sure their team has all of the campaign particulars they need.

It would be helpful to have everything on a Campaign Information Flyer. Campaign kickoff date (start date), turn in date, turn in location, approximate delivery dates, pick up location and time, forms of cash accepted, incentives or prizes, group goal, suggested personal sales goals, and other items mentioned based on conversations with your distributor. See The Key Leader's Kickoff Letter section later in the book.

Phase 3 – Campaign Sales (2-3 weeks, but no longer than 4 weeks)

Conduct your fundraising campaign and secure sales. Remember to instruct your Fundraising Team Members on the types of payments you will accept and to always receive full payment at the time of sale. Have a system in place for them to check in each week with their Team Leaders. Alert all Fundraising Team Members each week of the scheduled Turn In Date and location.

Phase 4 – Turn In (1 week)

Have your Collectors ready on the selected date and location for the turn in. After the money and order sheets are collected, your Chair will then prepare the Final Order Form and submit the order to the fundraising company or distributor.

One week should be plenty of time for all Team Members to turn in their money with order forms, count the money, put the money in the bank, prepare your Final Order Form with the proper products needed and finally turn in your order to your fundraising company or distributor.

This week will also give you some leeway for those few desperate stragglers who come in after the official turn in date. Inevitably, after the due date, you will have a few who misplaced their sales order forms and/or lost the money (checks or cash) and then ask if they can still turn in their order.

Of course, you should never announce you will have an extension after the official turn in date, but you may wish to have a system in place just in case.

Rather, it is for those few who call, "I really, really, really need to turn my orders in. I know I'm late, but I misplaced the order forms and have just now found them. These customers are expecting their items to be used as gifts."

Phase 5 – Product Processing And Delivery (1-3 weeks)

Once you've placed your order with your Fundraising Company, you now wait for your items to be processed and shipped to you.

There are three options of helping the fundraising company process the order to be shipped, depending on what has already been discussed with your distributor or fundraising company.  Check in the ***Student Packing*** section for more details, but here they are:

1. Bulk Shipping - Student Packing Needed
2. Bulk Shipping - No Student Packing Needed
3. Ship straight to the customer's home

Shipping items that are pre-fabricated like 'flags', should be able to ship rather quickly, usually arriving within 2-4 business days after the order is placed.  For more shipping timeframes, see the section on <u>Delivery Time</u> in the **Shipping And Handling** section.

Be sure to place your orders in the morning so they'll have the full day to be processed and your order entered into the computer for fulfillment.  Don't wait until 3pm on Friday to turn in your order and expect Friday, Saturday and Sunday to count as days against your delivery time.  Your order will likely not be reviewed for processing until the following Monday or Tuesday.

Phase 6 – Product Distribution To Customer (1 week)

If ordering in bulk, the final phase of your Product Brochure Fundraising Campaign is to give your Fundraising Team Members about a week to pick up their previously sold items at your group's Product Pick Up Day and then distribute to their customers.

<u>The Introductory Letter or Parent's Letter</u>

As a part of your brochure fundraising campaign you may need to use an introductory letter (or Parent's Letter at schools) explaining the details of your campaign.

Using an introductory flyer or "Parent's Letter" is highly overrated, but it is sometimes useful when you have children involved so that responsible adults know that your campaign has kicked off.  There is an example in the **Tools And Forms** section of this book which you may personalize by inserting your group's own information in.

For schools, the Principal's Office passes these flyers onto teachers who then, turn around and give out one per student to take home and show their parents.  Usually, a sales brochure and order taker form accompanies the

Parents Letter and prompts the parents to begin their fundraising efforts on behalf of the student.

This letter is not used particularly for "selling" the items as much as it is to provide key information to keep everyone on track during the campaign.

It should have several items highlighted in this one page flyer:

- School Name Or Organization Conducting The Sale
- Kick Off Date
- Goal Amount
- What Types Of Payments Will Be Accepted (also, what name should checks be made payable to)
- Payment In Full Due At Time Of Order (no COD's or partial payments)
- Chairperson's Contact Information (Name, Phone, email)
- Turn In Date (you must state emphatically that no orders can be turned in after this date… Use strong language like "No Exceptions", etc.)
- Instructions On How To Proceed With The Sale
- What The Group Is Expecting To Achieve (new playground equipment, student trip, new computers, etc.)
- Shipping Timeframe (participants should alert customers that it may take 2 to 4 weeks for delivery after the Turn In Date or end of the campaign)
- Thanking Each Participant Ahead Of Time For Their Efforts

If you elect to send a "Parent's Letter" by email, make sure you indicate any clickable links to areas you wish them to review.

- PDF of the sales brochure
- How they can share with others through social media.  Clever students have created a 1-3 minute video explaining the program and their parents' then email to friends and family or place in social media.
- Create your own Microsite with Homestead.com, TotalSnap.com or Pinterest.com and showcase your products and how to order.
- If available from your Fundraising Company, call attention to your group's exact online ecommerce Fundraising Website where they can buy the products (note: this same Fundraising Website link can also be spread effectively through social media and emails).

Make sure that you personalize these letters to your school's or nonprofit group's own personality.

# Safety

Addressing child and student safety is of paramount concern these days. Ideally, because of internet fundraising on the increase, door-to-door solicitation safety issues are naturally becoming less of a concern.

However, when conducting face-to-face sales it is always good to have safety rules in place for all to understand and abide. I would suggest going one step further by alerting the local authorities (mayor's office, police, 911) that you'll be conducting a neighborhood sale on the date you plan to conduct it. If for no other reason, a citizen should be able to check to confirm whether the fundraiser is legitimate or a scam.

Many years ago while I was a Cub Scout, I sold Scout Expo tickets around our neighborhood. I was always alone and rode my bike through the neighborhood without any concern for my safety. It was virtually unheard of during the 1960's for children to be molested by predatory adults. My parents certainly did not see my safety as an issue.

Well, it's a different day and one can only look on the internet for maps of registered sex offenders in their neighborhood to know that you can never allow your children to go out alone conducting a fundraiser.

I personally think that the days of door-to-door fundraising sales are just about over and should be avoided. Sales made by Fundraising Team Members should be mostly made through people they know or with accompanying adults at busy spots in the city.

It is better to have parents take sales material to places of work, stand outside of public places, calling relatives by phone or using Skype, have a booth set up at a fair, offer products at a mall or super store or use internet technology to conduct sales.

Here are a few rules which must be followed if your group does decide to conduct face-to-face sales.

1. Students and children should NEVER sell fundraising products alone. They should always be accompanied by another person and be supervised by an adult in visual sight of their activities at all times.

Even if a youth is standing outside of a grocery store in heavy trafficked area, you must have one or more adults present. It was always a rule to have at least two adults present with any Scout outing I was involved with, just in case of an accident allowing one adult to take the youth to the hospital, leaving the other adult with the remaining Scouts.

2. Only conduct activities in areas that are well known by the membership and parents.

3. If neighborhood selling occurs with youth involved, then their parents should always have an address or area proximity enabling them to know where to reach their child in case of a family emergency. They should always have a cell phone number and contact name of the adult in charge.

4. Only conduct sales during daylight hours and never at night.

5. Youth should be cautioned to never reveal personal information about themselves (phone number, family name, hobbies, etc.). If any customer needs to speak with anyone about the sale, then it is suggested the youth give their adult leader's name and phone number which should be listed on their Sales Order Form.

6. Fundraising Team Members should never enter into anyone's home for any reason. All transactions can be quickly conducted at the door.

7. Train your participants to alert the adult in charge if they feel threatened, frightened or uncomfortable with a customer's actions. The adult can then determine if further action should be taken by alerting authorities.

# Sales Incentives And Prizes

If you're wondering whether sales incentives actually increase sales, the answer is a definitive 'yes'. Prizes and sales awards are a great way to build excitement and competition in any fundraising campaign. The main goal; however, is to boost your fundraising profits.

Now the big question is what kind of prize or sales incentive to offer. For adults, you will want a more mature offering versus one that is more toy-oriented for students or youth. You may even want to survey your organization's members to see what interests them most.

For large organizations like schools, you may be able to negotiate with your fundraising distributor or supplier to provide a prize program for your students at no cost to your organization. The prizes are usually prominently shown by sales volume levels in a colorful flyer which is provided free for each student.

In most of these prize flyers it starts off showing plastic items for low level sales and moves to more expensive items like MP3 players for those levels requiring higher sales volume. The cost for these prizes may be figured in to the sales picture for free or your group may have to pay for them out of its profits so be sure to ask the fundraising company or distributor about these costs.

For example, you may be charged an extra 3% to 5% from your profits depending on the prize program you select. Rather large organizations or schools could receive this free if it is included as a part of their packaged agreement with the fundraising company selected.

For adults and teenagers you will do well not to offer "plastic junk" toys like those offered in most prize brochures. Instead, try providing a more practical incentive like a store gift card, prepaid credit card, restaurant card or similar.

Increase sales and participation by having a way for everybody to "win" something. Just be sure that you reward those who do the most sales by offering them the greatest prizes or incentives.

Even for only one item sold, I suggest you offer a small incentive for the Fundraising Team Members to achieve. Perhaps something special or something of minimal value like a special restaurant coupon from a local merchant that may be provided to you free or at a reduced charge.

By highlighting achievement levels for one item, five items, 10 items, 20 items, 30 items, 50 items, 100 items and finally 500 items or more you will definitely increase sales which leads to more profits. All the while, increasing the quality and/or value of the reward as more sales are made.

And don't get too cheap on the items you offer for higher sales levels achieved. Provide items that are seen as valuable for higher sales.

## Example of an incentive program presented at a typical Middle School.

The Principal gives an introduction of the fundraiser over the intercom and notifies all of the parents the first day. Each student takes home a flyer to their parents highlighting the sales incentives available to achieve. Each class will have a goal thermometer displayed showing their Group Incentive to motivate and show progress. Here are a few incentive examples:

- ✓ Every student who achieves his or her personal goal of one item sold is rewarded (only goal achievers can participate) by attending a silly hat day... get an extra recess time... receive a free desert card from the cafeteria... or other.
- ✓ Students selling 2 or more items will be entered into a "special drawing" to receive a special prize. Every additional 2 items sold will be given another entry.
- ✓ Students selling 3 or more items will be allowed to go to a watermelon feast.
- ✓ Students selling 20 items or more will receive a Limo Ride to a special event.
- ✓ The top student will receive a $25 iTune gift card.
- ✓ The top class with the most items sold will receive a pizza party.
- ✓ Every class with 100 sales or more will receive a popcorn party.
- ✓ Every Friday the principal will update the classes on their progress toward the goal.

## Offering Prizes From A Novelty Company

Novelty Companies can offer another inexpensive way to build a prize chest for pushing participants to achieve a personal goal and beyond. You should insure there is an actual flyer or brochure which shows all of the prizes available at each specific sales level.

It has been shown that these sales incentives really do work. Those interested in achieving prizes or incentives are typically the "high achievers", so why not help spur them into action.

Naturally, it is well worth having the prizes available for everyone. You may be surprised at just who turns out to be big achievers for these special prizes. They will likely do whatever it takes to get that special prize or incentive if they desire it.

Most Novelty Companies also have the flyers and brochures available with preset items and what it takes to achieve them. These flyers cost from 10 cents to 25 cents each, but a distributor may pick up the tab on these, because it means increased sales.

Here are a few novelty gift and prize companies to consider. These novelty prize companies have specifically been involved with the fundraising industry for many years. Some offer Prize Brochures and others offer many inexpensive items that will allow you to build your own Prize Brochure or Prize Flyer.

Novelty Inc. – www.noveltyincwholesale.com  or call 1-800-968-7442

Oriental Trading Company – www.orientaltrading.com  or call 1-800-875-8480

Rhode Island Novelty – www.rinovelty.com  or call 1-800-528-5599

Star Awards – www.star-awards.com  or call 1-800-837-7827

Tectron International – www.funareus.com  or call 1-323-588-9165

TGP Rewards – http://tpgrewards.com  or call 1-800-838-4550

Toy Network LLC – www.manleytoy.com  or call 1-800-767-9998


Prizes offered to individuals are often awarded in two ways, so be sure to find out which plan is being offered.

1. Tiered Rewards are where a series of more expensive items are offered for increasing sales levels achieved. As increased sales occur, the participant is moved to a higher tier or level where a group of more expensive items are

offered. The items offered in the previous tier cannot be claimed and are dropped out in favor of the more expensive items which can be claimed.

2. Cumulative Rewards occurs where participants who reach each sales level can claim items at that sales level and subsequent sales levels. For instance, if a participant has reached the Level 5 Sales Level he gets to select and keep 5 different prizes… one per level achieved.

Personal Sales Incentives

There's another way of boosting personal sales volume by offering sales incentives other than prizes. Using the catalog or brochure from your Fundraising Campaign, you may wish to make the very items shown, in the brochure, as prizes available for achieving a certain amount of sales volume.

For example, a small ladies church group sells candles to raise money for their mission project. They certainly weren't interested in the plastic gimmicks or toys, which student fundraisers offer, for their sales incentives.

So for their sales incentive promotion they offered each Fundraising Team Member one candle for every 10 candles sold. The 9 oz. candles sold for a retail price of $10 and the wholesale cost the group paid for the candles was $5 each not including shipping. So basically, when a Fundraising Team Member sold two candles, the group could actually afford buy an additional candle as a prize and still make a profit.

They gladly stretched the sales incentive to offer a free candle for every 10 candles sold. It was well received and actually pushed sales beyond their expectations. For their free candle, the Fundraising Team Member could also choose the actual candle scent they specifically wanted.

You will need to price the cost of your sales incentives so that you don't lose money.

Fun Personal Incentives Or Prizes

Personal Incentives or prizes that are fun include:

For each 10 units sold or for $50 in sales the participant gets…

- To Choose One Item From Current Sales Catalog
- A Movie Pass

For each 40 units sold or $200 in sales the participant receives a...

- Chance at a "Dash For Cash" (Cash Whirlwind, Cash Scramble)
- $25 Gift Cards
- $25 Store Cards

For each 100 units sold or $500 in sales the participant earns a...

- Silver Dollar
- Big Event / Sports Tickets
- $50 Cash
- Chauffeured Limousine Ride

## Inexpensive Personal Incentives

Personal Incentives that don't cost much might include:

- ✓ Picture taken with a sports star or local celebrity and framed.
- ✓ Baked Goods (iced brownie, fancy cupcake, kettle popcorn)
- ✓ Fancy dinner with a celebrity (Mayor, Bank President, Business Owner, Sports Star)
- ✓ Lessons Coupon (computer-how-to, tennis or golf, cake decorating, etc.)
- ✓ School Coupons (No Homework, Extra Ice Cream, Extra Recess)
- ✓ Boss For The Day (students can be "Principal For The Day" complete with announcements, proclamations, special treatment, special lunch, etc.)

## Early Bird Incentives

Personal "Early Bird' Incentives are used to help ramp up sales quickly. These incentives have to be within reach for sure, but they will help you accomplish some really fast sales.

Early Bird Incentive examples are:

- "During the First Week Only our Early Bird Prizes will go to all persons who have met their personal goal of selling 10 items."
- "We will be having daily prize drawings to all participants who have sold at least two items and turn in the sales results to their Team Leader each day. All will have a daily chance to have their name drawn."
- "For the first seven people to achieve $100 or more in sales, they will each receive one _____ (item)." *You can make it $200 or whatever you want to reach this level.*

Make sure these Early Birds are issued more sales order forms if they are required to turn in their first forms early. This will allow these "go getters" to continue making some great sales for you.

Other Individual Participant Incentive Ideas

A. Grand Prize Drawings

Here's another way to increase sales with personal incentives. Have an entry for a Grand Prize Drawing – For every 5 items sold, the Fundraising Team Member receives one ticket to be placed in a special drawing for a Grand Prize (TV, bike, MP3 player, game system, etc.). You buy this item from the money you've raised. This is above and beyond their normal achievement level incentives.

B. Corporate Sponsors

Solicit corporate sponsors, merchants, or retailers for this one big item and make a big deal about who is giving it away. Merchants understand that anything which attracts people to their stores will mean more sales as a result of that attention.

Well known company names also help create legitimacy to your fundraiser that really resonates with the public and Fundraising Team Members.

C. Merchant Coupon incentives can also help increase sales. Here are a few which could be relatively inexpensive or free depending on your arrangement with the merchant:

- ❖ Bowling Centers
- ❖ Skating Rinks
- ❖ Sporting Goods Store
- ❖ Fast Food Restaurants
- ❖ Miniature Golf Courses
- ❖ Movie Theatre Tickets
- ❖ Music Stores
- ❖ Anything which inspires and rewards your participants to achieve a certain sales level.

D. Public Recognition

Offering public recognition to those who reach a certain level is a great way to "pat them on the back" by allowing the community to learn about their efforts. Here are a few, but your Team Leaders can come up with more unique recognition for your local area.

- Lunch with the Mayor and a proclamation made.
- Dinner with a sports celebrity with picture placed in newspaper.
- TV, Radio or YouTube interview of those who've reached their goal and what it will mean for your organization.
- Conduct an Awards Ceremony at your school or organization where recognition occurs in front of their peers. Take pictures with the Group President or School Principal shaking their hands and place in the next group newsletter.

Dispersing Incentive Funds By Individual Effort

There is an age old problem of dispersing funds fairly where participants need to raise funds to attend an event or help pay for their trip.

How do you disperse funds fairly for use by your group's members? Did all of the members of your group work equally in raising funds?

Many leaders have faced the problem of being fair about dividing the funds raised with those who put in the proper amount of work vs. those who did practically no fundraising at all.

Here's an example: A member of your group rarely shows up at fundraising functions, but is a part of your scheduled group trip or activity you have planned. Should you provide for their attendance equally along with others who were putting in more work toward the fundraising efforts? Certainly not!

Another member is at every fundraising activity and even involves their parents as helpers. Who should get the biggest chunk of the pie to pay for future activities? The answer is obviously the member putting in the most effort. They should be rewarded the greatest for their hard work.

The Solution: Half of the funds raised by a group member goes into the overall group fund and half goes toward the individuals account as kept within a separate Individual Account Summary. The Individual Account Summary (**IAS**) will record the sales made and/or hours the individual and parents worked on fundraisers.

The IAS can be used to separate the cash amount of items sold.

Example #1: A high school choir sells candy bars for 50 cents each. The candy costs the choir 20 cents to buy. Their profit of 30 cents is divided in half with 15 cents going to the general choir account and 15 cents placed under a member's IAS.

Example #2: A church youth member with the help of her parents sells 200 candy bars and is credited with $30 toward her mission trip. Be sure to allow parents to help sell at their place of business and among their acquaintances.

Example #3: A high school band will be playing at a college football bowl and decides to sell candles to raise money. They receive 50% profit from the sale of $10 candles. The band student gets $2.50 for every candles sold toward paying for his personal trip expenses. The group also gets $2.50 toward the overall expenses.

Division By Dues Given: Organizations that charge membership dues may want to establish this same principle for their members. For example, scout groups may charge $1.00 per meeting to help defer expenses for badges and awards.

Creating an account for paying for badges may help maintain a fair accounting for those keeping their dues up to date versus those who rarely bring their dues.  This will encourage responsibility from both scouts and their parents when paying their fair share of the dues.

Hourly Division Examples:  A church youth group raises $1500.00 at an 8 hour car wash.  A particular church youth member works all 8 hours at the car wash and his parents, also in attendance, work 6 hours each.  The youth member has 20 hours credited toward his IAS.

Another youth member worked only 6 hours.  There were 8 other members and 4 other parents who worked an additional 124 hours for a combined total of 150 hours.

Half of the $1500 goes into the general fund for a planned missionary trip.  The remaining $750 is divided up among the participants.

Divide the $750 by 150 hours and you get $5 per man hour worked.  Therefore, the youth with 20 hours of work will be credited with $100 placed in his IAS.  The youth with 6 hours of work will receive $30.

This greatly adds to your workforce by rewarding those really wanting to work.  It also encourages parental involvement by crediting their child for their work as well.

A Few Rules:

Rule #1 -- If a member quits the group or moves during mid-year, then they relinquish any money that went into their IAS.  These monies will revert into the group's general fund.

Rule #2 -- Make it clear that each IAS is only good for a given year or activity.  After the current year lapses or the special activity ends, then all IAS monies revert into the general fund.

You may establish alternatives and allow funds to be carried over from one event to another during a given year.

The key is to make fundraising participation fair without penalizing an individual because of something that is beyond his or her control.

Use these principles early on and it will prevent misunderstandings and problems with fairness in the future.

Just remember to make this policy clear to all parents and youth through flyers, announcements, and consistent reminders as the events you've planned draw near.

## Qualifiers For Groups To Achieve A Certain Incentive

Let's not forget to have some friendly group competition with a "Biggest Prize" winner.

Your Biggest Prize could be achieved by the fundraising team with the best customer acquisition, class with the most money raised, club with the most items sold, or other level reached by the top achiever.

You've heard of prize winners announced as "the group with the most fundraising product sales gets to..."

> ➢ Have A Pizza Party
> ➢ Wear A 'Wild Wig' Special Day
> ➢ Go Out For Ice Cream
> ➢ Dress Up Crazy All Day
> ➢ Join Our Watermelon Bash
> ➢ Participate In The Barbecue Grill Out Day
> ➢ Take A Trip To The Ball Park
> ➢ Splash At The Pool Party
> ➢ Receive A Hamburger Supper
> ➢ Go On A Field Trip
> ➢ Take A Day Off

There are endless numbers of special ways to push any group or team to go beyond the normal goal and beat other teams for the Biggest Prize.

You must publish or announce these incentives to Sub-groups within the larger organization or league such as individual teams, classrooms, Cub dens, Scout patrols or other.

For example you may announce that:

- Chapters with 50% participation or more get...
- Dens with 75% participation or more earn...
- Groups with 100% participation receive...

- Classrooms where students sell at least 2 items each, teachers will receive $____ to be used for _____.
- Teams where each Team Member reaches their personal goal will receive _____.
- The class achieving the most sales will receive…
- When the school reaches its Funding Goal the Principal will…(Kiss A Pig, Shave His Head, Eat A Worm, etc.).

These group incentives could be something silly like "throw a cream pie in your boss's face… your coach's face… your organizer's face…"

Or it could be a more serious item like the Pizza Party mentioned earlier. You'll just have to decide what incentives you want to offer.

# Shipping And Handling

Most everybody has shipped items by US Postal Service, UPS or FedEx so there is not much of a learning curve here. There are a few details you should consider as you plan your fundraising strategy.

As you may be aware, shipping is not available to Post Office Boxes except in rare cases. Most shippers only deliver to physical addresses. So make sure that you provide a good "shipping address" when placing your Final Order.

Also, make sure your items can be delivered where they can be received immediately or will remain secure until you arrive to pick it up. I've heard of a few disappointed individuals who had their chocolate bars delivered to their front porch. Some had the bars melt, because they were left out in the weather and some were picked up by thieves.

I would finally point out that most products are only delivered in the Continental USA. It's unfortunate that the shipping costs to Guam, Alaska, Puerto Rico, Hawaii, U.S. Virgin Islands and international locations will absorb all of the profit in delivering to those areas since shipping is so expensive.

If you live in those non-continental states or US territories, I would recommend conducting a fundraiser like Pizza Discount Cards, Scratch cards, or similar non-food product which can be sent fairly cheap by USPS Priority Mail or any rush delivery package. Your other option would be to use a Home Delivery or Online Program like those already discussed.

Now, let's look at other information you may need to consider.

## Free Shipping vs. Paying For Your Shipment

Many times larger orders are shipped free by the fundraising company to you when reaching a certain sales threshold. Medium sized orders may have S&H (shipping and handling) shared by the company and you.

Smaller orders typically have shipping costs passed on to you unless otherwise noted. You may be charged for shipping if; for instance, you only order 10 candles or 15 individual snacks. Most candy bar orders have free shipping included with each case shipped.

You will also likely pay a little bit more for items delivered in a residential area rather than commercial so don't be surprised if you are asked which one the delivery location is situated in.

## Packing and Handling

More and more suppliers with food items, which might melt due to heat issues, are now shipping items packed in dry ice so that your products are delivered fresh and in the best condition possible. Inquire with your distributor or supplier if they use dry ice. When handling dry ice be sure to take appropriate precautions when unpacking items.

For large orders of frozen cookie dough or ready-to-bake gourmet food which requires baking, you will need to secure enough refrigeration space until you can have your Fundraising Team Members pick up their sold items. Ideally, you should have this location secured before starting your fundraising campaign, but definitely before placing your Final Order with the fundraising company or distributor.

The larger the order, the more a loading dock will be required. Expect to pay extra if you do not have a loading dock, forklift available, or if the delivery man is required to use his own equipment to unload. It helps to have a strong crew of helpers ready to help with the unloading if you have a large order.

## Verifying Delivery

It is your responsibility to verify that a shipment is accurate and complete when it arrives. After the delivery truck has left and you find your order is not accurate, then you will be held responsible for additional delivery charges that occur later to deliver the missing goods.

It becomes particularly important for larger orders to have a small team of adults available to do some counting and checking the packing slip which accompanies the order.

Accurate checking of your order is vital, because many times refunds or returns are not accepted once you sign for your order.

Immediately, notify your distributor or supplier to replace a broken or damaged item when discovered. Ideally, refusal of damaged packages should be done at the time of delivery.

In many cases damaged or broken items legitimately noted at time of delivery can be shipped out immediately by your supplier, taking very little time to arrive and distribute to customers.


## Delivery Time

Most of the time, orders will take less than a week to deliver to you, but don't count on Overnight Express or rush deliver to be offered. Even if you do have the option to get your order within 1-2 business days, you will pay so much extra money for shipping that you will potentially lose any good profit you plan to make.

One of the few exceptions to ask for rushed delivery are items like scratch cards or restaurant discount cards which can be inexpensively sent in a small package.

I always tell customers to expect delivery within 14 business days. Many times those deliveries will arrive sooner, but it all depends on where you are in the queue with your order being packed and when the trucking company picks up the order from your fundraising company for shipment and the distance you are located from the warehouse.

With food orders most fundraising suppliers will stress it could take 12 – 16 business days for delivery. Cookie dough, popcorn and snacks are usually made fresh taking time to prepare so don't expect these items to be waiting in stock which could be pulled from a shelf, pack and send off to you quickly.

There is a huge optimum freshness concern for foods manufactured at most fundraising food product companies. The items they make are much fresher than those found at the grocery store or a member warehouse club.

Items like candles which are pre-made and can be stacked for future sales, can be packed within a few days and shipped to you so that you receive it between 5 – 7 business days.

Delivery of 1 to10 cases of chocolate bars usually takes from 3 – 5 business days for you to receive it. Now, if you turn in your order late Friday afternoon, don't expect your delivery to go out before the following Monday or Tuesday.

Of course the larger the order, requiring a pallet to ship, the longer it will take to arrive.

## Fuel Surcharge Fees

Fuel surcharge fees added to your bill is one of those "gotcha" deals. You will usually know ahead of time if this happens, but you may not until you get your total invoice. This is not the fault of your fundraising distributor or supplier, but rather is passed on by the trucking company.

Fuel surcharge fees don't amount to much anyway and are usually on the scale of a few dollars for small orders. For larger orders these costs could add up, so make sure that you find out about any fuel surcharges when you place your Final Order.

## Examples Of Shipping Fees

To give you an idea of what some shipping scenarios are, let me cover a few below. This is by no means definitive and you may begin to realize it is all calculated on weight. Your fundraising company may absorb some costs.

- ❖ Chocolate Bars – Under 10 cases are mostly free or cost under $40 for less than $1,000 ordered. Shipping during summer months may be as high as $10 per case due to special refrigerated carriers needed.

- ❖ Scratch Cards – $20 for orders of less than 100 cards.

- ❖ Candles – $55 for 100 candles

- ❖ Coffee And Gourmet Beverages – $100 for 150 packets

- ❖ Merchant Cards – $15 for orders of less than 100 cards

- ❖ Decorative Yard Flags – $15 for 50 flags

- ❖ Two Year Planners – $10 for a case of 60 planners

- ❖ Dry Baked Goods And Mixes – $50 for 200 items

# Tax Issues

It is apparent that local sales taxes and state sales taxes are increasingly being imposed on nonprofit groups.

I frequently hear nonprofit leaders say that their organization is "tax free" and exempt from paying any taxes. They may have an IRS 501(c)3 determination letter which exempts them from paying federal taxes, so they tend to lump all taxes under that banner.

You should never assume your organization is "sales tax exempt". Sales taxes are different than state or national income or corporate taxes. More than likely you will still have to pay sales taxes on items unless the money given to you is an outright donation of cash with no strings attached.

Each state has different tax laws to consider. Check with your local taxing authority or go to www.fundraisetaxlaw.org which shows each state's Attorney General guidance on which nonprofits are allowed to conduct tax exempt sales fundraisers.

As a fundraising professional, I am not in a position to provide tax advice since I am not an attorney or CPA; therefore, I recommend that your organization use a qualified accountant to handle your tax issues.

As it is, tax laws are continuously changing so they will have to be reviewed from time to time to keep current.

Let's take a look at a few tax issues you may have to deal with.

- **Individual Customers Paying Taxes** – Individuals making a purchase from your fundraising sale are not "tax exempt" so they are required to pay sales taxes just like they would if making a purchase through regular commerce channels. You may decide not to charge each individual customer, but rather handle the taxes collectively, taken from your profits made.

  It may be necessary to pay sales taxes on fundraising products even if your organization or school is sales tax exempt. Most of the time when your organization has a sales tax exemption, it means that the merchant, whom your organizations buys from, does not collect taxes from your group on purchases at their marketplace for supplies, furniture and such.

So be clear on this issue by going to your state's Department Of Taxation website where these sales tax regulations are spelled out and even explains how much each municipality requires you to collect. Make sure you determine whether you will pay taxes on the retail you charge others or on the wholesale price that the fundraising supplier charges you.

Many fundraising products which are promoted and sold online are now collecting the necessary sales taxes at the time of the sale for you, taking the hassle out of requiring you to collect those sales taxes from individual customers.

- **Local And State Sales Taxes** – As stated, most groups are not exempt from local or state sales taxes. You should check with your local taxing authority first to determine if you will need to pay local or state sales taxes. Some states have a website (see www.fundraisetaxlaw.org/states.html) dedicated to showing all tax rates for each county, parish, or city in its state. Most states allow you to pay direct through the state and it will be forwarded to the local taxing authority, but a few states require you to pay state and local taxes separately. To do this you must fill out the necessary application forms with the Treasurer's Office or the Sherriff's Office that collects taxes.

- **Federal Taxes** – If you are a 501(c)3 organization, registered with the IRS, then you are not normally required to pay federal taxes. For more on this see the IRS Website www.irs.gov. You may be a smaller entity (chapter) in a larger organization (national parent organization) which has this status, so make sure your national parent organization knows that you are conducting this fundraiser under their authority. If you don't have a tax exempt status, then any revenue created may be charged against your group. Make sure you check with your CPA or Tax Attorney to guide you through the process. It may be advantageous for your group to sign up with the IRS and get your own

501(c)3 designation if you don't currently hold it.   Please note that this does not allow your supporters buying any fundraising products to then deduct their purchase amount as a donation, since they are receiving something of value when they make a purchase from your organization.  All funds raised on behalf of your 501(c)3 tax-exempt organization must be controlled and used solely by your organization to support the activities of your organization.

- **Unrelated Business Income Tax** – If you are a 501(c)3 organization or under the umbrella of a 501(c)3 organization, then you may also be required to pay an UBIT (Unrelated Business Income Tax).  Basically, the UBIT is income your group does not customarily make money from as a fundraising mechanism. Again, check the IRS Website for the latest rules on this.  If in doubt, it may be advisable to add your specific fundraiser into your organization's bylaws and/or official minutes to make sure it becomes a part of your normal fundraising plans.  I advise you to get with your CPA, Tax Attorney or Accountant about the UBIT.

- **Token Items Offered For A Donation** – Basically, anytime you offer something of substantial fair market value for a donation, then the actual value of the item must be deducted from the actual donation before being used as a tax deduction.  The exception is if your group offers a "token" item to a donor who is "insubstantial" (coupon, candy bar, mints, single flower, etc.).  Token items allowed by the IRS typically include those with the organization's logo or name on them (coffee mug, t-shirt, pen, etc.).  At this writing, these token items must not exceed a value of 2% of the donation or $91.00 whichever is less.  For example, a 7 oz. $10 Candle is clearly worth more than 20 cents (2% of $10 = $.20).  Therefore, avoid the Tax Deductibility issue on products and simply declare, if asked, that it is a "product fundraiser" with no tax deductions available.

# Student Packing

As mentioned earlier in this book, there is a situation that will save groups a lot of time as you prepare to distribute the sold items to your customers. It's called Student Packing.

This is an industry term referring to pre-packaging each Fundraising Team Member's order, allowing for effortless pick up by a Fundraising Team Member (or Student) being labeled and ready in one bundle to distribute to their customers.

A fundraising supplier will pre-sort all merchandise by overall Group Level or League (school), then by Team Level (or class), and finally to individual Fundraising Team Member (student) all labeled accordingly so that the Team Member can simply show up and pick up their bundled items.

This feature is extra handy for large schools and organizations of at least 100 Fundraising Team Members who makes several sales each. It is not really necessary for members who average sales of one to two items.

Student Packing is also great if you have only a handful of volunteers who have each made a couple dozen sales each. It helps separate a huge bulk order into smaller quantities for each Fundraising Team Member.

If you need your order packaged for each student or Fundraising Team Member then you will send a copy of each individual sales form turned in for the sales they generated.

The fundraising company will then separate these orders as they enter them into the computer for fulfillment and when packed will label the team members name on each package for easy distribution on the Customer Product Distribution Day.

Because this method requires someone at the fundraising company to physically key the orders into a computer, it will take up to several days longer to process your order and get it shipped. It will also have an extra cost added.

Remember, your other option for processing your order is to have "no student packing" necessary. So, if you are not concerned about having your order pre-separated for each Fundraising Team Member, then you will simply turn in one consolidated order to the fundraising company and separate it later when the bulk shipment arrives.  You will then not need to send each individual sales form for each team member in since you will be separating it by participants yourself.  This insures your order is processed and shipped faster.

It is very important to stress to all Fundraising Team Members to make sure all sales order forms which they turn in are legible.

Before your campaign begins, you should stress to everyone when filling out the form that they legibly spell out the customer's name and contact information making sure when writing to press hard enough to reach through a triplicate form so that each page can be read.

This is especially important for items shipped straight to the customer's home address or when a personalized message needs to be spelled exactly as written.

Most Student Packing is offered at a rate of 5% deducted from your group's profit.  If you were expecting a 40% profit, then you will receive 35%.  Why the extra expense?  Well, warehouse packagers trained specifically for this task will need to be paid by the fundraising company.

Sometimes fundraising companies will often offer this service free to larger groups of 1,000 or more in order to close the deal over their competition.  Just don't expect it for free if your group is smaller.

# Bookkeeping Principles

In this section I will give you a game plan for keeping track of the money your group raises. You will need an accurate paper trail for money received.

This is crucial so that you protect yourself from any scrutiny which could come your way and for creating a positive accountability record should evaluation by others become necessary.

Let's cover the basics. You will need to set up a plan for the following:

1. Recruiting Some Help
2. Instructions To Your Team Members
3. How To Receive Money On The Turn In Date
4. Depositing Funds
5. Payment Deficiencies
6. Preparations Before Making The Final Order

Let's look at these in more detail.

## Recruiting Some Help

You may want to have one person head up your bookkeeping job and call that person your Accounting Chair or Bookkeeping Manager. It would be nice to recruit someone with banking or accounting experience to help make this a smooth part of your fundraising structure.

You will also need at least a couple of people to help get the job done, but you may need more to help supervise the final collection, counting, posting and depositing of your funds.

I suggest you have 3 to 6 individuals for larger organizations available during the counting process if possible. If available, none should be from the same household for obvious reasons of integrity.

Having others involved will keep anyone from questioning a single individual for the monies received. Even if you are a small group, you should have at least one other person involved with this process to protect all concerned. It will also help you catch any counting errors which might occur.

## Instructions To Your Team Members

Many times your product fundraising company will have instructions on how to instruct your Fundraising Team Members to collect funds. If not, you can use the following when collecting funds:

- ❖ Only take complete payment for the items the customers buys. Don't accept orders with a promise to "pay you later" when the product comes in.

- ❖ Use a Money Collecting Envelope to place the collected checks and cash in when received. This will help keep from losing money. Your fundraising product company may have these for your group to use.

- ❖ Make sure they understand there will be no orders accepted after the turn-in-date (day after the sale ends).

- ❖ If accepting checks, make sure all know who to make checks payable to so that they may instruct their customers.

- ❖ Make sure each Fundraising Team Member gets legible contact information written on their order forms by their customers.

## How To Receive Money On The Turn In Date

At the location on your turn in date, a table should be set up so that two or three Collectors can handle orders for more than one individual at a time. These Collectors can count the money and review the Sales Order Form and then pass it to another person or two who will do the "auditing" or double checking their figures. This will keep the process moving along at a steady pace. Each person should place their initials on the Sales Order Form to certify their involvement.

The Collector should review checks showing the correct amount which corresponds to the amount shown on the Sales Order Form according to the number of items ordered. They should be sure that it is made payable to their group with the Fundraising Team Member's (or Student's) name appearing in the "For" spot at the bottom of the check. This will help in identifying where it came from in case the check bounces.

I have heard of some organizations creating a "Locked Drop Box" for students or participants to place their monies into, but this still leads to one or two people who have the key; thus, placing them in a precarious position if the funds are short when the orders are placed in the box. I would avoid this type of system, because you may not have a box large enough.

An alternative turn in method, if you have a Weekly Sales Incentive Program taking place, will be to have a table set up at the end of each week for a 4 hour period. Perhaps between 3pm to 7pm would work.

At the end of each order receiving and money counting day, your Treasurer may have in place a method established to keep track of funds generated and spent so make sure they are an integral part of all financial transactions. The Treasurer may be using an accounting program like QuickBooks to handle your transactions so make sure you are doing everything to mesh with your group's system.


## Depositing Funds

After you have gathered all orders and monies you will want to make a total counting. When doing so, it will be easy to use an adding machine with a paper printer ticket capability.

Assign someone to make sure that all checks are payable to your group and endorsed on the back of the check with your stamped Account Number and Checking Account Name on the reverse or "For Deposit Only".

You may elect to wait a couple of days after depositing your funds and before placing your Final Order with your fundraising product company in case there are insufficient funds that occur from bounced checks. This will allow you to adjust your final product count to match what you will pay to the fundraising product company.

Use adhesive paper straps supplied by your bank to bundle different denominations together. Place the monies with an accounting of each denomination from the counting tape from your calculator into a secure bank money bag with a lock.

You will need two people in one vehicle to take the currency bag to your bank. These two may want to be followed by another for safety reasons particularly if you are dealing with large amounts of money. Several vehicles at a bank drop will help deter any potential theft from outsiders.

If making weekly or daily deposits, you should make your deposits at unpredictable times during daylight hours if possible.

## Payment Deficiencies

Finally, I want you to guard against payment deficiencies or bounced checks. Take this seriously without delay, because the longer you wait to collect, the harder it will be to get it corrected.

The best way to avoid payment deficiencies is to only take cash or credit cards. Of course only two forms of payment will limit sales since there are a lot of people who only use checks and still don't trust giving others their credit card information. And accepting cash only could lead to a "borrowing" problem by parents and others before it gets to the group.

If you think taking "cash only" is the only way to operate, I will tell you that I personally oversaw a huge popcorn fundraising sale where "cash only" sales were the rule. With over 750 adult volunteers involved, there were a dozen cases where people were turned over to law enforcement for theft from their own local group's sales efforts. Cash is very easy to "borrow" (steal) from any sale.

They were just going to "borrow" the money to get them through a tough personal financial situation and at some point it became evident they could never repay the money. Many of these "borrowers" simply assumed the money would go unnoticed.

This is the reason that the future of fundraising will move progressively toward the Fundraising Product Website sales model which will allow each supporter to make secure transactions with their credit card online. There is a list of some good online fundraising programs at FreeWebFundraiser.com.

If a check does bounce, here's what you should do:

1. Ask the Fundraising Team Member or one of your adult 'Collectors' to contact the customer and ask for cash to cover the item cost and replace the check. Try the phone number printed on the check or information found on the sales order form.

2. Contact the bank shown on the check and ask if there are sufficient funds for you to run the check back through a second time.

3. If you have difficulty reaching a customer not being responsive by phone, then the next effort to secure the insufficient funds would be to send a certified letter requiring a signature by the recipient. Firmly state in the simplest terms that their check was presented for payment and was insufficient. Give the check number, amount, date written and so forth. State clearly that they have ten days to send a money order, cashier's check or can pay by cash before they are turned over to authorities. If the bank has charged an insufficient funds fee, then pass this cost along to the customer and state this in the letter. Keep a copy of each item sent.

4. Reluctantly, you will need to determine if you want to "write it off" as a bad transaction or to take legal action and go to small claims court. If you do go the legal route, then you will need to bring copies of all of your records dealing with this customer.

Preparations Before Making The Final Order

The last leg of your bookkeeping will be to place the Final Order with the fundraising product company. Usually this is done by mailing in one form with the composite number of products needed separated by item numbers. If your group is using a triplicate order form, then you will want to send two copies along with the order and keep one for yourself. If your group is using a single page Sales Order Form which needs to be sent in for Student Packing, then I suggest that you make a copy of each order form before sending it in by mail or express delivery. You may realize by now that things really do get lost in the mail, so make sure you create copies of documents mailed.

You should be aware that you most likely will be required to pay Sales Taxes by your state and local taxing authority unless exempt by law. See the section earlier in this book about Tax Issues.

If you collected sales taxes, you will now need to file a return for the amount collected. Have your treasurer take care of this in a timely manner.

# Turning In Your Order

Turning in your order may be one of the most crucial aspects of your fundraising sales campaign process. Emphasis should be placed on legibility and accuracy as you prepare your final order to your fundraising company.

The duty of turning in a final order usually falls to the Fundraising Campaign Chair since this person was the one who made contact and arrangements with the fundraising company or distributor in the beginning.

Turning in the final order to your fundraising company is very simple. Use the forms which the fundraising company has provided for you. That way it will mesh with the way they normally process an order for the fastest delivery possible to their nonprofit customers.

For simple sales most companies supply a single page Fundraising Sales Order Form for your Fundraising Team Members to use and then you later consolidate these into one Final Order Form (also referred to as a Tally Sheet or Master Tally Form).

Some fundraising companies will provide a triplicate sales order form for your Fundraising Team Members to use. Many times the company will use these triplicate order forms to tally your order if they need exact wording for a custom gift (like personalized holiday cards with envelopes), shipping the items to the end consumer's home address, or preparing it for Student Packing.

As you prepare your order using triplicate order forms, you keep one of the colored copies and send the top white original along with the other colored copy in with your order. There is no need to tally a Final Order Form since the triplicate order forms are scanned using a fulfillment software program to maintain the exact order needed and even broken down by the piece and coded for each participant.

Here is the process your final order will take:

1. The Fundraising Team Member, along with others on the team, turns in his or her money with sales order forms to the designated Collectors on the turn-in-date.

2. Make a copy of each member's Sales Order Form – one for your records to keep and one to be used by the member as the items are distributed to their customers.

3. All money is deposited in your group's bank account.

4. The Fundraising Campaign Chair or designee tallies every item by making a list of all products ordered by customers with a breakdown by Product Number (SKU #) if there is one and/or Item Description (flavor, scent, color, etc.).

5. The number of each Product Number is recorded on the Final Order Form along with the retail price of each and then totaled. Make a copy for yourself and send one in with your order. In the end, this will give you the final retail sales figure which your distributor will then use to settle on your profit earned. (retail sales – wholesale cost of the items the distributor charges you – shipping and handling – any taxes = Profit Due your group).

6. Fax, email or mail your order in and send the amount due to your product company, distributor or fundraising company. Pay by credit card, with one check from the group's bank account or by money order.

7. The distributor will confirm the order amounts and money due to fulfill the order and give an estimated time for your order to be filled and the approximate time for your shipment to arrive.

Ask your Fundraising Distributor for enough Fundraising Sales Order Forms (one for each Fundraising Team Members to mark down customer orders) and Final Order Form (to turn in your order) if you haven't been supplied with these.

Keep these thought in mind as you anticipate turning in your order.

✓ Expect to pay the fundraising company for your products before your items are shipped out to you or your customers. Fundraising companies or distributors rarely extend credit anymore or allow COD.

✓ Plan to pay with one check from your organization's bank account. Distributors or Suppliers will not accept individual checks from your customers.

✓ Your group already has their retail money collected so there should be no problem paying the wholesale rate plus any taxes, shipping and handling required. The difference between the two is the actual profit which you can start using immediately.

✓ Only schools can insist on being invoiced instead of paying for their order upfront. Extracurricular groups or school clubs do not apply, because it is difficult to "run down" adult sponsors not tied to a permanent business address if an invoice is not paid on time.

✓ On-The-Spot sales products (like candy bar sales and restaurant cards) do not need to be tallied since these items are ordered and paid for upfront.

✓ Be sure to check with your fundraising company at the time of order to determine if you need a "loading dock" or if they have a ramp on their truck.

✓ Keep copies of all forms turned in by your Fundraising Team before anything is sent to the fundraising company or distributor.

# Distribution Of Products To Supporters

Delivery of products to your Supporters (your customers) is of utmost importance and should be completed in a timely manner. When I say "timely", I mean within a few days after the bulk order has been delivered to your organization. Really, distribution should occur within a couple of days after the pick-up-date.

Timely delivery will make all the difference when going back to these same customers next year and asking for their support. Here are a few details to review to prepare for the proper distribution of products to your Supporters.

Receiving Your Shipment

- Secure one delivery address to "ship to". Make sure you have space for warehousing the items in a protected location. If being delivered to a large school or company location, you may want to get approval in writing and signed by the person in charge of the location (CEO, Principal, General Manager). This avoids any problems the day of delivery if there will be other people involved in accepting the delivery. You should be able to show that person the delivery arrangements already approved so they will go ahead and accept delivery.

- Refrigeration for frozen items requires special consideration so make sure you have an industrial freezer available.

- Will your shipper need access to a "loading dock" or will they have a ramp on their truck? Will they have access to a forklift or will they need to bring their own? Some shippers require a loading dock or they will not deliver. Don't expect the driver/shipper to manually unload your shipment for you. You should expect to have several helpers in good physical shape with dollies or have access to a forklift.

- Go back and notify workers and leaders through the "chain of command" of an approximate time of delivery. This will cut down on confusion for both customers and fundraising workers.

- Expect up to 14 business days for your bulk order to arrive. Don't pre-set a pick-up-date unless you've done this before and know the exact ship time.

- Have helpers ready on time for unloading at the assigned delivery location. Your delivery shipper should be calling the number and contact person they were given when you placed the order. Once delivery time is confirmed, this contact person should then call the helpers with the approximate time to arrive. Make sure you have a 5-6 hour window of time blocked out since most delivery times are not precise.

Distributing Your Shipment

Now that the order has arrived, you have two methods to get the product to the customer:

1. Have the actual customer personally pick up their product at a certain distribution location during a certain time frame.

2. Have your Fundraising Team Members pick up the items they sold and then personally deliver to the end-customer.

Here are some thoughts you may want to take into consideration.

- For refrigerated products, remind the customer that the products should be placed in the freezer as soon as possible. You may want to hand out a flyer that states this.

- Stress timely pick-ups. Give between four and six hours for adequate pick-up time. Make sure you offer some of the time outside of normal business hours. Perhaps from 2pm to 8pm.

- As items are picked up, check them off of your list by those responsible for picking up the products. As the final hour or two of the delivery day unfolds, to prevent "no shows", you should have phone numbers handy and give these people a quick call. For remaining items, have a delivery contingency plan ready, especially for perishable food items.

# After The Campaign

Your group has now conducted a successful fundraising campaign and has done a fantastic job selling a particular product. Now you can kick back and relax, right?

Well, not so fast. There is still the "Thank You" phase that must (I said MUST) be completed. It's a basic part of good customer service and it WILL enhance your continued good standing in your community especially in relation to next year's fundraiser.

You will need to express your gratitude to...

- ✓ Fundraising Team Members
- ✓ Customers

Thanking Your Fundraising Team Members

1. Make a list of all of your volunteers. I know this sounds simple, but by writing the names down and their accomplishments during the campaign helps in properly acknowledging everyone for their contribution.

If you've ever been to a meeting where the announcer forgot to mention someone and then has to come back... a little embarrassed... and report on those additions who were not given a proper 'thank you' during the main announcement, then you know how awkward it is not to be fully prepared.

2. Recognize those volunteers (your Fundraising Team Members) in the most appropriate fashion possible. You may also want to highlight their accomplishments by also showing their actual sales made. This can be done by:

- Having a theme related party, luncheon or dinner where only the successful Fundraising Team Members are invited (pizza party, ice cream social, watermelon feast, etc.) who reach a certain goal.
- Announcing participants in the organization's newsletter or taking out an ad in the town newspaper.

- Making a sign listing all of the volunteers with their sales accomplishments and posting it in a prominent location.
- Send out a special email to all supporters and donors.
- Post pictures and names of participants on your group's website.
- Send an acknowledgement from your organization's Facebook, Pinterest or other social media site (showing photos and listing names of all participants) and goal achievers.
- Offer a personal call from the President or Executive Director of the organization.
- Send a personal handwritten note from the Fundraising Campaign Chair.
- Place a 'Winners Circle' wall up in a prominent place listing the top fundraisers, top sellers or high achievers highlighting the dollars raised and their accomplishments.
- Send a 'thank you survey' asking for their help to make the next effort better (people love to give advice and it makes them feel more a part of something that is lasting).
- Thank each helper by phone call, letter and/or email from the Fundraising Campaign Chair.
- Recognize top performers at the next meeting or membership gathering.
- Present certificates to those who achieved a certain level of sales and participation.
- Have a chance to enter the "Money Whirlwind". You've probably seen these contraptions from rent-a-centers with dollar bills circulating inside a clear booth as people try to grab dollars. My daughter once did this when she was 6 years old where a new bank branch was opening up in the area and she grabbed $50. It is fun, motivates participants and requires very little money. It also makes them want to participate in the next fundraising event.
- An alternative to the Money Whirlwind would be to have a "Prize Coupon Jump" where you've secured food and other items from local merchants. This could be ice cream cones, pizzas, toys, sandwich combos, etc. Give them 30 seconds to grab as many as they can.
- If conducted through a school or youth organization, reward parents in some manner. For example, when conducting a candle fundraiser, I always allowed the top performing 2-3 parents to choose a couple of candles each at no cost to them. It was an inexpensive way for them to choose their own candle scents indicating that you value their assistance enough to allow them to personalize their own reward.

- Teachers who had at least 50% participation from their class should receive something free (e.g. a Wal-Mart gift card). Perhaps with a 75% they might get to wear pajamas to work or 100% participation they receive a ride in a limousine to work with big fanfare. You can have up to 6 individuals ride in any one day.
- Lunch with the boss, lunch with a local celebrity (mayor, sports star, business owner), or lunch with the principal at a fancy spot could make the difference to a participant.

For students at a school it might be a good idea to post their names on bulletin boards, their names displayed up-and-down the hall on colorful placards, list names on cardboard bricks and displayed as a 'wall of honor', have their names called out over a loud-speaker, honor each student with a certificate at an event or during the lunch hour, or anything that will properly thank them for their efforts and encourage their participation the next time.


Thanking Your Customers

Do you want your customers to become true supporters? Ones who help you financially, again and again?

Then you must make it a priority to make them feel special by thanking them. Do this with sincerity and quickly after the campaign has finished.

It's not just appropriate to express appreciation to your customers or supporters, it is absolutely essential to thank them. If nothing else, a simple "thank you" by telephone call from the Chair goes a long way to getting them to support your organization the next time around.

With any contact, be sure to convey the results of your fundraising campaign. Show these supporters how their efforts have made a big impact and they will readily entertain the idea of becoming a partner with your efforts.

Thank supporters often, as many times as you can. Make them feel they have truly been helpful, generous and making a difference for their community or interests.


Here are a few ways to let them know how they are special:

- Have your Fundraising Team Member call them and thank them for their order.

- Have one of your officers call them and thank them for their support.
- Have one of your members or someone that you are financially assisting send a note of appreciation (this allows for a strong emotional bond to be made with your supporters).
- Have your Fundraising Team Leaders send handwritten notes of thanks. Handwritten notes are becoming scarce and because of this, they have a greater impact these days.

Some supporters may tell you that "it was nothing", or "save a stamp and don't bother sending me a 'thank you'", or "it was no big deal", but don't believe them. They are merely being courteous and deflecting any form of selfishness. The truth is that all of us desire to be appreciated.

Be sure to send them a note with a link to your website so they can order more product if they want to. Send them a note of gratitude with a business card indicating your fundraising website address for them to reference.

Or send them a "thank you" note by email with the website link and suggest how they can assist you anytime of the year by ordering more products.

You'd be surprised at how many times customers call back and ask, "I'd like to purchase some more of those _____?" With money on the table like that, you'd be wise to keep communicating your fundraising website link again and again.

Just remember to always offer them an opportunity to help again. People really do want to be asked to help… so, ask them often. Let them tell you when "enough is enough". I doubt you will ever reach that point.


## Keeping Proper Track Of Your Customers

Have you ever heard the expression "the list is gold"? It's a phrase that marketers use, because the best future customer is one who has already bought or has been supportive in the past. In other words, it takes a lot less effort to sell to a former customer than it does having to expend the effort to find a new customer.

One excellent way to keep track of customers and supporters is to build a list. This customer list will end up saving time when the next fundraising campaign is conducted. It should be accessible and portable so it can be able to be passed on to the next Fundraising Campaign Chair or President.

Software programs like Outlook, Excel, Microsoft Access, QuickBooks, or FileMaker Pro, to name a few, can really help. More specifically, you can utilize contact managers like ACT!, Goldmine, and others. Open Office (http://www.openoffice.org/product/base.html) has a good free contact manager.

There are also many good online accessible programs like Pimex, E-Z Contact Book, Free Address Book, and more available at CNET.com (http://download.cnet.com). For sharing online with others get the ScheduFlo Multi-Location software.

Specific fundraising contact management software is available free or at a cost of a few hundred dollars. My favorites include DonorPerfect.com, CharityFinders.com, eTapestry.com, DoJiggy.com, and Convio.com.

My advice to you is to find a donor database or contact manager of some sort, even if it costs you a little money, because you will likely recoup the cost many times over by re-engaging a former happy supporter who could add more funds to your program each and every year.

# The Structured Fundraising Campaign For Large Groups

This segment is designed for larger organization's needing to implement an effective structured fundraising campaign. It will show you how to manage a full volunteer staffed fundraising team which you'll need to get the "big bucks".

So why is there a need to have a Structured Fundraising Campaign as opposed to just letting all of your members "go out" and find some customers? Well, let's look at why a structured campaign is superior to a typical fundraising campaign.

A Structured Fundraising Campaign insures success because...

- A contact list is created to use as a base structure in reaching customers.
- Every Fundraising Team Leader participates by buying a product.
- Every Fundraising Team Member participates by buying a product.
- Every former customer is contacted and asked to buy products.
- New customers are added by each Team Member who could also buy products.
- Fundraising Team Members is asked to give a report to team leaders; thus, applying some peer pressure to proactively push each to reach their contacts in a timely manner.

The one thing that I know will NOT work is that YOU, as an individual within your nonprofit group, "try to do it by yourself". I've seen it so many times how one person tries to take on the whole burden for achieving the funds needed.

You are rolling out a dynamic fundraising campaign, so you will need to share the load and utilize your resources to the maximum by recruiting helpers.

At first you will need to evaluate whether you have enough volunteers early on as you establish your fundraising campaign. If you do not have enough volunteers to carry off the procedure described below, then I would suggest requiring your Team Leaders, who you've recruited, to recruit their own Team Members as volunteers. These new volunteers do not have to be members of your organization, just that they have a strong desire to help out and see their participation through to the end of the campaign.

As with any fundraising campaign, you will need to secure a Fundraising Campaign Chair to head your fundraising effort. This person may also be referred to as Chairman, Chairperson, Coordinator, Fundraising Director, Fundraising Coordinator or simply Chair if you prefer to use any of those titles.

The Fundraising Campaign Chair is someone who will only head this specific fundraising campaign instance during the year. This Chair is not the same person who heads your yearlong fundraising program usually called the Fundraising Committee Chair or Ways And Means Committee Chair.

To establish a campaign structure (see page 123) you will also need Team Leaders to help you. As your fundraising team grows in size, it will require the recruiting of Team Leaders (sometimes called Team Captains). Within these larger campaigns, each Team Leader will be in charge of a handful of Fundraising Team Members who will help carry out their part of the fundraising campaign.

With this campaign method, contact of previous customers should be maximized while reaching out to new supporters (new customers). Overall, this structured campaign will reach out to 1. Members (current and past), 2. Past Supporters, and 3. New Supporters.

All members of the organization (including your Fundraising Team) will be asked to participate as well with the goal of a 100% Participation distinction. It doesn't matter if they buy one or ten products from your product brochure or online webstore, as long as they buy something, then they are counted as participating. This buying requirement from participating fundraising workers will insure for a successful campaign.


The Structured Campaign Game Plan

A structured game plan for your campaign is designed to reach all of the members of your organization first before reaching out to your community.

It is deemed "structured" because unlike the typical non-structured Fundraising Campaign which most schools typically conduct, your Fundraising Team Members first start by contacting the organization's membership before going out on their own and find customers within their own personal social network only (family, friends, neighbors, co-workers).

If you are the Chair of a typical school fundraiser and you wish to have a Structured Campaign, then you may consider each Teacher or Room Parent as a Team Leader and proceed from there. Each Team Leader can then recruit 3 – 7 parents of students within the class to be Team Members and contact the rest of the families of the room as prospects. Use the '**Use Product Brochures'** section if you do not want a structured campaign.

A Structured Fundraising Campaign will bring many of your group's members together as volunteer Team Members. There is heavy emphasis on the proper recruitment of your team. Job Descriptions for each position can be found at the end of this book.

You will notice the structured campaign has a military type chain of command. This is designed to spread the work load over many people efficiently, so that very little effort is done by each while creating a tremendous outcome collectively. You will want to adapt it to fit with your membership structure.

If you are a small organization of less than 100 members or have not done too many fundraisers, it might be desirable to initially use the simpler general fundraising plans highlighted in this book.

Campaign Timeline

A campaign timeline is necessary to keep every Fundraising Team Member on target.

By this point you will have already selected your products and the fundraising distributor or supplier who will be working with your group. You have also worked out with them any details like profit you'll receive, what product brochures you'll need and other basic information previously discussed.

This timeline is not complicated, but will show everyone how to allocate their time in quickly reaching the final objective of full participation.

➢ **PreCampaign – Weeks One and Two**: a.) Order from your fundraising company any brochures and sales order forms you'll need; b.) Recruit your Team Leadership and Team Members starting in Week One; c.) Prepare information for every member of the Fundraising Campaign Team; d.) The Fundraising Committee gathers member and contact names into a Contact Manager database or list; e.) As each Team Leader and Team Member is recruited, they should immediately purchase one or more items for themselves from the product brochure or through the organization's Fundraising Product Website if one is available.

> **Campaign Kickoff – Week Three** – Assign 4-6 prospect names, previously generated, showing contact information, to each Team Member (handed out at the kickoff or emailed to them). Hold this 30 to 60 minute meeting and hand out any materials (brochures, sales order forms, etc.) with instructions for every Team Leader and Team Member.

Use the sample *Key Leader's Kickoff Letter* found in the **Forms And Tools** section of this book. It should be stressed that each Team Leader also agrees to act as a 'working Team Member' by contacting people too. You don't need 'supervisors' – you need workers!

> **Week Three** – Each Team Member makes their contacts for this week and next. Each should average a minimum of 1 to 2 calls per day. Ideally, it would be better to have a face-to-face meeting with the contact to show the actual product brochure, but if a physical meeting is not feasible, you may also be able to call and walk the contact through the fundraising product website if your group has one or through a PDF of the product brochure if posted on your group's website.

I've known of innovative Team Members who have faxed the product brochure and sales order form or have emailed a scanned brochure (in PDF format) and then called the person to get their order. They have used a brief introductory note similar to *Fundraising Introductory Letter From Nonprofit Members To Friends* found in the **Forms And Tools** section.

Team Members report to their Team Leaders at the conclusion of each week with a report of their contacts made and the results of those contacts. Team Leaders give a report to the Campaign Chair or Division Chairs if part of a larger effort. Division Chairs report back to the Fundraising Campaign Chair who is then informed enough to make adjustments in the campaign where necessary.

> **Week Four** – Team Members continue calling on the remaining contacts assigned to them. They also start reaching out beyond the contact list to their own family, friends, neighbors and co-workers and ask for their support. This adds to your growing list of supporters. I recommend giving special prizes or incentives to the top 10 or 20 Team Members who bring in the most new supports.

Team Members report to Team Leaders. Team Leaders give a report to the Division Chairs. Division Chairs report back to the Fundraising Campaign Chair who is then informed enough to make adjustments in the campaign where necessary.

> **Week Five** – Team Members and Team Leadership begin turning in results of their fundraising efforts. Team Leaders should remind all Team Members of the Turn In Date and location. Each is encouraged to finish up any leftover actions or calls. The Chair charts the results on the Thermometer Goal Chart (example in this book).

> **Week Six** – Conclude all activity and finalize the Thermometer Goal Chart. Keep copies of all individual sales order forms before sending to any fundraising company. The Chair turns in the order to their chosen fundraising company.

The Fundraising Committee meets and analyzes the outcome. A report is sent to all Division Chairs (if any), Team Leaders and Team Members about the outcome; the estimated shipping time given by the fundraising company; the approximate product pick up time; and product pick up location.

> **Week Seven** – Send letters of appreciation to everyone (including all Team Members, Team Leaders and Customers) for their part in making the campaign a success and report on the amount raised (retail prices – wholesale cost = amount raised).

➢ **Week Eight And Beyond** – As your product shipment arrives, alert your team of the time and location for products to be picked up. Each Team Member then picks up their customer's products and delivers to them within the next few days.

Developing A Campaign Contact List

In planning your fundraising strategy, you'll need to identify who you will contact and ask to participate with the Fundraising Product Campaign. This is crucial and will eventually maximize your funding potential by focusing on contacting the right people during the campaign.

Your Fundraising Committee should be the group most involved in creating your customer contact list. Your list may consist of:

❖ Current Membership List
❖ Current Donor List
❖ Participants From Your Group's Past Events
❖ Inactive Members
❖ Supporters From Past Functions or Events
❖ Community Groups Your Organization Is Connected With
❖ Newsletter Recipients
❖ Alumni

Your Campaign Contact List should be compiled into one database. You may need to take notes on each prospect so you'll know how to follow up with those individuals who ask to be contacted again. Your organization should use a computerized contact manager like ACT!, Microsoft Outlook, OpenOffice.org BASE, GoldMine or similar program to properly store your contacts and their comments.

For those who decide not to participate NOW, make arrangements to contact them again later using some of the fundraising methods in this book. Just because someone chooses not to participate initially, does not mean they will not consider signing up later as the campaign progresses and as they see positive results from what others are experiencing.

Build your list to include your campaign leadership who should be asked to be the first to participate. In fact, once any leader is recruited he or she should immediately become their own first customer. In turn, as their Team Members are assigned to them or recruited by them, these Team Members should follow suit and become their own first customer as well.

Each recruited Team Member should not be placed in the compiled list of supporters you'll use, so they'll not be needlessly contacted by another Team Member during the campaign.

Campaign Recruitment

As you might have noticed, the structured campaign is far from a simple fundraiser. It is essential that you recruit the right people for your team as you proceed. See the flow charts in this section for a visual perspective.

When recruiting the overall Fundraising Campaign Chair you should choose a person with good standing in your organization and the community.

The **Fundraising Campaign Chair** has the responsibility to recruit 2 to 7 Division Chairs and/or Team Leaders (sometimes called Team Captains). Recruit only Team Leaders, without any Division Chairs, if you plan on contacting less than 200 potential supporters in the campaign.

Each **Division Chair** will be responsible for guiding enough Team Members to contact 90 to 180 people. Each Division Chair is responsible for recruiting 3 to 6 Team Leaders to assist in the effort.

Each team should be designated with its own unique team name. You are not required to use the same names in the charts shown in the book (Lead Gifts, Advance Gifts, Sustainer Gifts, etc.), but can choose your own unique Division Names.

Each **Team Leader** in turn will be responsible for recruiting 5 Team Members each. This will mean each team is responsible for contacting 30 people from your contact list.

Each **Team Member** will be responsible for approaching 5 potential supporters (members of your organization and community prospects) from the compiled list your Fundraising Committee generated in the Pre-Campaign Phase.

This list will be made available and ultimately divided up so that everyone on the list will be contacted.

The campaign structure shown with three Division Chairs is for a compiled list of 405 people who will be contacted (remember the Division Chairs should also call on 5 prospects each).

If your compiled list is larger than this, simply add more Division Chairs to handle the work load. You should avoid going beyond 7 Division Chairs at one time, because it makes it more complex.

If your organization has less than 200 contacts on your list, the Campaign Chair simply recruits Team Leaders instead of Division Chairs.

A prospect list of close to 1,000 names (actual 945 names) would require about 7 Division Chairs.

If you have a compiled contact list larger than 1,000 names, you may want to recruit a Co-Chair and divide the list up between the two or you should start a new campaign a few months after the conclusion of the first campaign allowing you to contact another 500 to 1,000 potential supporters.

## Overall Campaign Structure

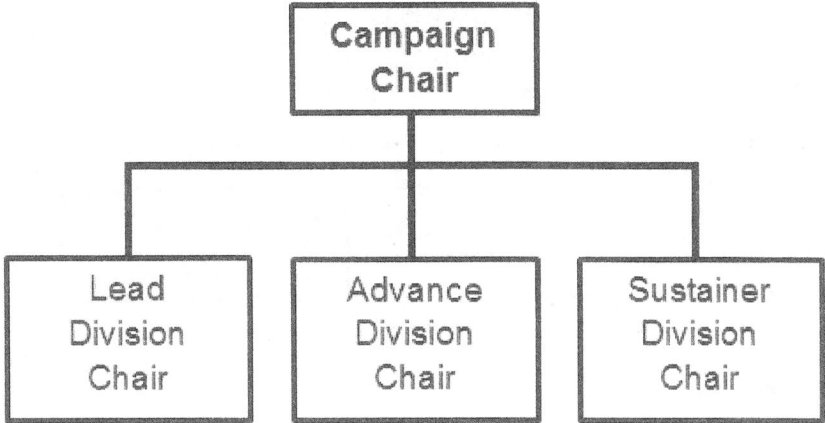

```
                    ┌──────────────┐
                    │   Campaign   │
                    │    Chair     │
                    └──────────────┘
            ┌──────────────┼──────────────┐
    ┌───────────┐   ┌───────────┐   ┌───────────┐
    │   Lead    │   │  Advance  │   │ Sustainer │
    │ Division  │   │ Division  │   │ Division  │
    │   Chair   │   │   Chair   │   │   Chair   │
    └───────────┘   └───────────┘   └───────────┘
```

## Team Structure

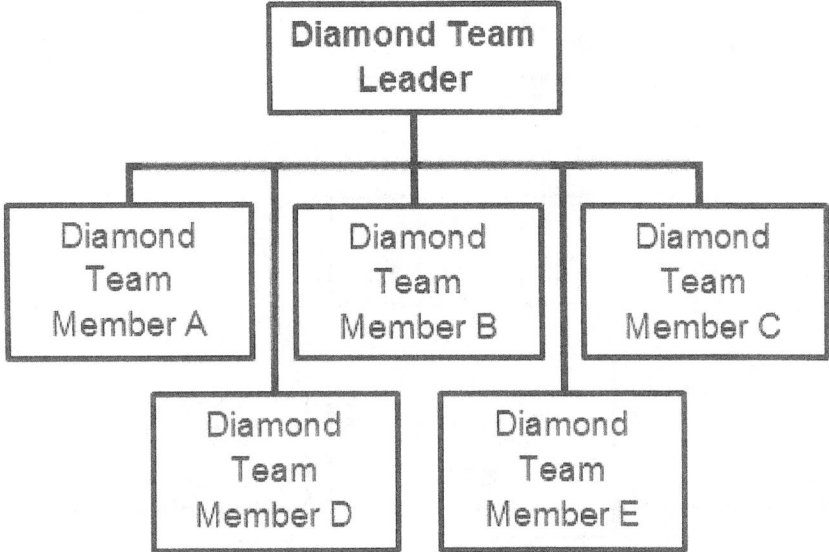

```
                    ┌──────────────┐
                    │ Diamond Team │
                    │    Leader    │
                    └──────────────┘
            ┌──────────────┼──────────────┐
    ┌───────────┐   ┌───────────┐   ┌───────────┐
    │  Diamond  │   │  Diamond  │   │  Diamond  │
    │   Team    │   │   Team    │   │   Team    │
    │ Member A  │   │ Member B  │   │ Member C  │
    └───────────┘   └───────────┘   └───────────┘
         ┌───────────┐   ┌───────────┐
         │  Diamond  │   │  Diamond  │
         │   Team    │   │   Team    │
         │ Member D  │   │ Member E  │
         └───────────┘   └───────────┘
```

## Divisions Structure

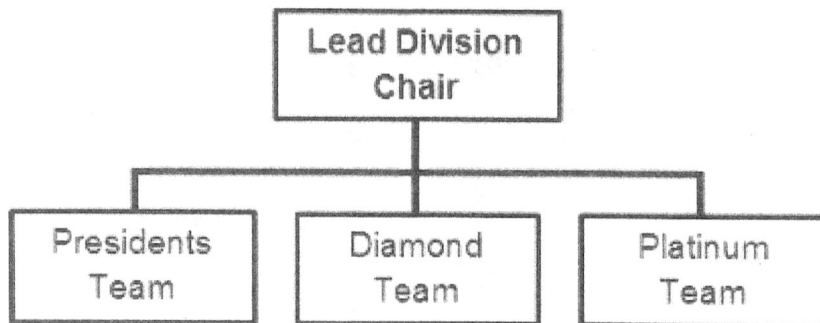

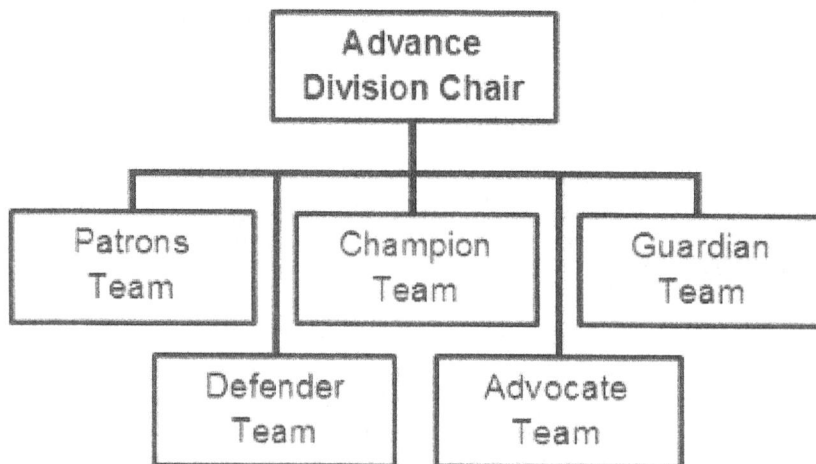

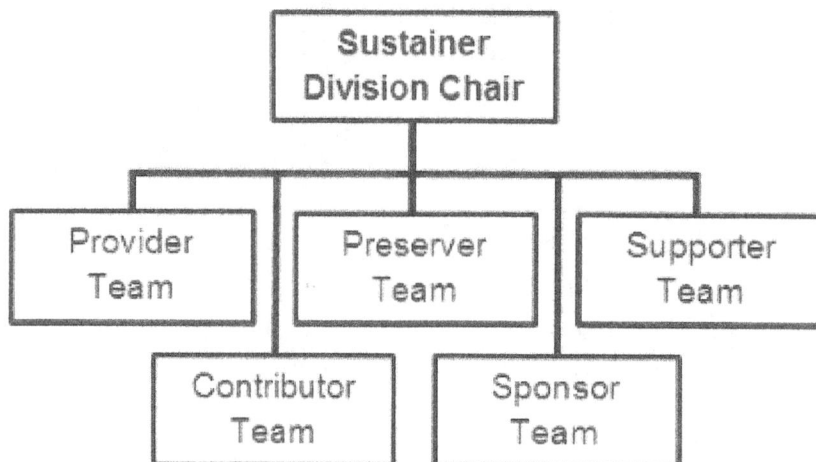

```
                    ┌─────────────────┐
                    │  Lead Division  │
                    │     Chair       │
                    └────────┬────────┘
          ┌──────────────────┼──────────────────┐
  ┌───────────────┐  ┌───────────────┐  ┌───────────────┐
  │  Presidents   │  │   Diamond     │  │   Platinum    │
  │     Team      │  │    Team       │  │     Team      │
  └───────────────┘  └───────────────┘  └───────────────┘


                    ┌─────────────────┐
                    │    Advance      │
                    │ Division Chair  │
                    └────────┬────────┘
       ┌─────────────────────┼─────────────────────┐
  ┌───────────────┐  ┌───────────────┐  ┌───────────────┐
  │   Patrons     │  │   Champion    │  │   Guardian    │
  │    Team       │  │    Team       │  │     Team      │
  └───────────────┘  └───────────────┘  └───────────────┘
          ┌───────────────┐  ┌───────────────┐
          │   Defender    │  │   Advocate    │
          │    Team       │  │     Team      │
          └───────────────┘  └───────────────┘


                    ┌─────────────────┐
                    │   Sustainer     │
                    │ Division Chair  │
                    └────────┬────────┘
       ┌─────────────────────┼─────────────────────┐
  ┌───────────────┐  ┌───────────────┐  ┌───────────────┐
  │   Provider    │  │   Preserver   │  │   Supporter   │
  │    Team       │  │    Team       │  │     Team      │
  └───────────────┘  └───────────────┘  └───────────────┘
          ┌───────────────┐  ┌───────────────┐
          │  Contributor  │  │   Sponsor     │
          │    Team       │  │     Team      │
          └───────────────┘  └───────────────┘
```

Recruiting The Fundraising Campaign Chair

The most crucial phase of the Structured Campaign is the recruitment process. This process will take two to three weeks to complete, but will lay the groundwork for a fast flowing campaign once underway.

Begin by recruiting a Fundraising Campaign Chair and sharing this game plan with him or her. See the Job Description for the Fundraising Campaign Chair in the **Tools And Forms** section.

When recruiting the Fundraising Campaign Chair, you must ask this person to set the example and become the first product customer themselves.

Asking the Chair to be the first to purchase a product is a benchmark in any fundraising campaign.

It's called "Leading By Example" which has been addressed already.


Action Plan

1. The Fundraising Campaign Chair looks through the organization's member list and makes a list of 7 to 10 people who would be good prospects as Division Chairs (or Team Leaders if your campaign contact list is smaller). The Division Chairs (or Team Leaders) must be organized and energetic individuals willing to help recruit and report back to the Fundraising Campaign Chair each week. The Fundraising Campaign Chair should first know how many members they will contact through this campaign and then divide the number up into the appropriate number of Division Chairs from his/her compiled membership list.

2. Once the Division Chairs are recruited, each will make a list of 7 to 10 people who would be good prospects as Team Leaders. The Team Leaders must be organized, well known individuals willing to help recruit and report back to the Division Chair each week. With the help of the Fundraising Campaign Chair, the Division Chair should recruit enough Team Leaders so that each team is able to reach about 30 potential customers from your compiled contact list. Each team has 5 Team Members contacting 5 each and the Team Leader contacts 5 which equals 30 prospects. So, if there are 150 prospects to contact for a particular division, the Division Chair will need

to recruit five Team Leaders.

3. Once the Team Leaders are recruited, each will need to make a list of 7 to 10 people who would be good prospects as Team Members. The Team Members must be organized, motivated individuals willing to make their 5 contacts and report back to the Team Leader each week. With the help of the Division Chair, the Team Leader should recruit enough Team Members. So if there are 30 potential customers to contact for any given team, the Team Leader will need to recruit five Team Members. Remember, the Team Leader contacts five too.

4. Team Members will each be assigned 4 – 6 names of potential customers to contact in a two to three week period of time. They should make weekly reports to their Team Leaders each Friday morning (or whenever designated by the Fundraising Campaign Chair).

Now here is a key component when each Team Member, Team Leader and Division Chair is recruited. The person recruited must agree to:

- Complete their tasks assigned in a timely manner.
- Report to their leader at the end of each week.
- Sign up as a customer first before they ask others. They should do this the week they are recruited and before starting to recruit others themselves.
- Be willing to ask others they recruit (any Team Leaders or Team Members) to also sign up as a customer when agreeing to serve.

This will mean at the end of your recruitment phase, that every Division Chair, Team Leader and Team Member will already be a customer; thus, having already raised money for your organization or school.

**Congratulations!** You have already achieved SUCCESS and have just built a powerful Product Fundraising Campaign in just a few weeks even before the official kickoff. This is more than 95% of other nonprofit organizations conducting a product fundraising sale have ever accomplished.

## Campaign Kickoff Meeting

There are two methods of holding a kickoff with your Structured Fundraising Campaign:

A.) Hold the kickoff in the morning or during lunchtime. Include a fast meal (e.g. donuts and coffee for morning kickoffs or box lunch for dinner meetings) and keep your team for no more than an hour with ALL Division Chairs, Team Leaders and Team Members attending...
**or**
B.) Allow each Division Chair to hold a smaller kickoff meeting for their own Team Members only (i.e. all of their Team Leaders and their Team Members).

## Typical Action Plan

1. Offer snacks or quick boxed meal at your kickoff meeting as your Fundraising Team Members arrive. Have your Thermometer Goal Chart on display in a prominent location (ranging about 36" in height). You may have to go to a copy center to get it printed in this size or hand draw it. Have a table near the entrance for each Team Member to turn in their own order as they enter if they haven't done so. Remember, part of the recruitment process is to secure their own purchase commitment as they agree to serve. If the recruiter (i.e. Team Leader) left a product brochure at the time of the actual recruitment, then this should be no problem.

2. After 20 – 30 minutes of people gathering and eating, have your Fundraising Campaign Chair (or Division Chair of a smaller kickoff) give a brief overview of what you hope to accomplish with this Fundraising Campaign. Be sure to touch upon what the money is being raised for and stress that everybody present will be expected to become a customer first before asking others on their list.

3. Always stress 100% participation by your team in purchasing at least one product. Reemphasize the "leading by example" model that everybody should follow. Whether you actually achieve your goal of 100% participation is beside the point – *you should still promote 100% Participation*.

Have the Fundraising Campaign Chair (or Division Chair) use a red marker and then place a mark on the "goal thermometer" showing their own participation and invite other leaders and members to come up to the podium to place their own mark (using a red magic marker) based on the earlier turn in of their own order. This puts "peer pressure" on all in attendance to complete the necessary task of purchasing their own product.

State the Campaign Timeline (outlined in this section) indicating when members should complete the sign-up phase. Give an actual final turn-in date. Because people have different pay periods (teachers and some government workers receive their paycheck once a month), give a minimum two week window for customer sign-ups after the contact is made.

4. Have your materials (product brochure, sales order forms, key leader's kickoff letter) ready to hand out to each Team Member. Ask each attendee to go home today and make their product selection or do it before leaving the meeting. Stress the "you can't ask others to do what you have not already done yourself" approach. Ask each person in attendance to offer to the group any testimonials or positive results which they have already experienced.

5. After materials are handed out, dismiss your group with the 100% Participation challenge.

Here Are Some Attributes You'll Need For An Effective Kickoff:

1. Always confirm the kickoff location with the CEO, Principal or person in charge of your desired location and anything else you will need for the kickoff like sound systems, microphones, banners, meeting space, chairs, head table, projectors, snacks, etc.

2. Have your products displayed, forms ready, fundraising goal thermometer, brochures ready in a visual presentation as your Fundraising Team Members arrive. Show any prizes available for them to achieve. Place your product display in a conspicuous place, such as up on stage or on the other side of the room, to avoid congestion.

3. Have your agenda ready so that you can refer to all of the items you'll need to cover, but also have a presentation script ready to read if necessary. You should state your name, position of authority, why you to raise money, campaign timeline and the sequence of events, and hold a Q&A for any

remaining questions the Fundraising Team Members might have. Make sure as the Fundraising Campaign Chair that you are full of enthusiasm and strongly emphasize the campaign timeframe, especially the Turn-in Date.

4. Continuously refer to your fundraising goal thermometer which is prominently displayed. State the personal minimum goal each Fundraising Team Member should achieve.

5. Have one of your Team Leaders speak about how to "sell" to supporters in the community. Use some of the ideas indicated in **The Easy Art Of Asking** and **Fundraising Tips For Beginners** sections in this book. Give some examples of how easy it will be to achieve their own personal sales goal.

6. Have a different Team Leader show and speak about the incentives or sales prizes available if any.

7. Create an orderly method for distributing the fundraising materials (product brochures, sales order forms, list of sales incentives, prizes, etc.). For schools, you should have the appropriate number of materials ready to hand to each teacher. For large organizations like booster clubs, these should be handed to parents as you check off their name.

The Meeting With The Prospective Customer

A meeting with prospective customers will involve either a 1.) Face-to-face meeting showing a product brochure, 2.) Telephone call while reviewing your Fundraising Product Website (if any) or brochure posted (as a PDF) online, or 3.) Telephone call while you review the brochure that was emailed or faxed earlier.

Here is a checklist for success for each campaign Fundraising Team Member:

- Buy one or more of the products offered through your fundraising product brochure before asking others to do so. This shows you are "leading by example".

- Thoroughly become familiar with the product brochure, sales order form and the Fundraising Product Website if any. After receiving your fundraising materials, contact the prospective customer assigned to you as soon as possible. Call or set an appointment for a visit. Use the sample script provided below, if setting an appointment for a face-to-face meeting.

- Be cheerful, friendly, and enthusiastic when speaking or meeting with your prospect.

- Remember, you are not "begging" anyone to support your group, but merely giving your prospect the opportunity to help your organization through this unique product fundraiser.

- Take the time to generate interest and excitement about your efforts. Do not use high pressure sales tactics. Show the product brochure and explain briefly how they can choose their product. Actually 'smile' while you are speaking, because your conversation will come across as more friendly and inviting.

- It is a known fact that two Team Members meeting with any prospect are much more effective than one alone, so pair up and take another Team Member if you wish.

Appointment Setting Phone Script

*"Hello, is _____ (Contact's name) there?"*

*"Hi _____ (Contact's name), this is _____ (Your first and last name) with _____ (Your organization). How are you doing? Great! Have you been notified about our new fundraiser yet?*

*(Wait for a response.)*

*Well, I've been recruited to help contact a few of our members and supporters this week to personally give the presentation about our fundraiser to them. I was asked to give you a call and make an appointment to meet you or visit with you by phone and give you the presentation. Is that possible?*

*(They should respond in the affirmative.) Good!*

*What would be the best time to visit with you this week? Anytime Tuesday or Thursday would be good for me. OK, we'll meet _____ (date) at _____ (time) at _____ (place). Call me at (xxx) xxx-xxxx if something comes up and you can't meet then. Otherwise, I'll see you there. Good bye."*

# Alternative Fundraising Campaign Plans

Now that we've reviewed how a Structured Fundraising Campaign works you may want to conduct a smaller alternative campaign plan or a unique secondary fundraiser which is not as structured as your main fundraising campaign.

If you're tired of conducting the same old typical fundraising campaign or need to shake up your efforts on a whole new scale and make them fun, then these alternatives may help.

Perhaps you have already conducted your normal fundraising campaign, but want to also reach out into your community gathering more support.

Well, I've got a whole bunch of alternative ways to conduct or enhance your next fundraiser using some fantastic alternative fundraising campaign plans.

Some of these plans offer super quick methods to kick start your fundraiser into high gear. In this section, you will discover many ideas for rapid success.

As I've discussed already, securing a Fundraising Committee is a crucial step to the overall success of your annual fundraising efforts. Otherwise, you could struggle in getting your fundraiser moving and wonder why it's not working very well.

It's because you don't have enough support from others. Remember, you can't do it by yourself.

A Fundraising Committee is designed to "share the load" while evaluating the fundraising process all year long. Ultimately, this committee is responsible for recruiting each Fundraising Campaign Chair as needed.

If you don't have a Fundraising Committee, then you may need to set one up. I've included a Job Description for your Fundraising Committee Chair and Fundraising Committee Members in the **Tools And Forms** section. It will help steer you into setting up your committee properly.

Take a look at the Year Long Comprehensive Fundraising Plan later on in this book. It is the most comprehensive alternative method to get started raising funds immediately on all levels.

Let's review some Quick Startup fundraising plans you can use.

**\* The Gathering \***

The Gathering approach is a simple means of making an announcement at one of your regular meetings or event gatherings. Nothing too complicated. Basically, your group's leader (or Minister, Executive Director, President, etc.) will announce that your group is introducing a new means of raising funds.

This method is used mostly by groups which do not normally conduct fundraisers or do not want a structured campaign.

It can easily be used by any individual who is not a member of the group, but who wants to help the nonprofit organization or school conduct the fundraiser through their own organizations efforts.

At the gathering, the CEO, should announce that their organization leadership is "so excited about the possibilities" of this new product fundraiser that a Campaign Chair has already been selected.

Stress that this fundraising product campaign will not replace regular donations, tithes or ongoing fundraising efforts being conducted by the organization, but will greatly enhance the annual financial resources with a new stream of funding for the organization.

Please do not get rid of any regular donation or funding programs at this point.

At the gathering, you should have on hand some product brochures or literature. Highlight the Fundraising Website address supporters should visit if there is one.

Simply pass out these flyers or brochures and ask each person present to go home and choose their products or logon to the group's Fundraising Website if they have one and help the group out by selecting one or more products there.

The flyers can also be folded and inserted into an Order Of Service bulletin at churches or worship centers or at any local Club meeting. Make sure it has your Fundraising Website address clearly marked and how to turn in the order if otherwise.

Action Guide

1. At your meeting, have the Fundraising Chair give a brief overview of what you hope to accomplish.

2. Always stress 100% participation by the group's members as a way of accomplishing your participation goal. Place a "goal thermometer chart" in a prominent place at the meeting if you want to set a participation goal. Set a timeline indicating when members should complete their orders. Because people have different pay periods (when they receive their paycheck), give a minimum two week window for supporters to order. Note: Your Fundraising Chair and Top Two Key Leaders of your organization should already have chosen their products by buying through a product brochure or the group's Fundraising Product Website if they have one.

3. Have your literature ready. Simply pass out the information and ask each participant to purchase an item now and hand it in to the Chair or to go home purchase items through the group's Fundraising Website.

4. After a couple of weeks, the Fundraising Chair should make or send an announcement about the progress of your group's fundraising efforts. Point to the Goal Thermometer Sheet showing your progress. Do this every week until you reach your participation goal.

**\* The Canvas Approach \***

Ask each of your members to take a handful of fundraising flyers or product brochures with an order form attached and hand them out to everyone they know around the community.

Anybody outside of your normal membership like neighbors, friends, office workers, and family should be considered.

It must be assumed by now that most of your membership has already participated and is a customer, are a little knowledgeable about the fundraiser and can share some of the merits of what is being accomplished.

You might also want to have a special day of the month where your members meet together for coffee and donuts in the morning and then go into your surrounding neighborhood to place the sales flyers on doors of homes and offices or just hand out at the shopping mall (with permission of course).

## Action Guide

1.  At a regular meeting of your members or Fundraising Committee ask for voluntary participation in helping to "get the word out" about your fundraiser. Make sure every member participating is on board as a customer first, because they will certainly be asked by people they meet, "Are you participating in the fundraiser?"

2.  Take one of the normal brochures or flyers supplied by your distributor and make plenty of copies of about 7 to 14 flyers per participant. You will place the sales order form on the back and include instructions on how to mail it in with a check made payable to the organization or how to order at the group's fundraising website. Make sure the website address is clearly displayed if you have one.

3.  Remind your members that each flyer has a full description about the products so there's no need to "hard sell" it to your supporters or those you meet. As each approaches a friend with the brochure and sales order form, a sample intro could be:

> *"Hi, Jane. How are you? Great!*
>
> *Listen, I'm helping my nonprofit organization (church, association, synagogue, ministry, club, etc.) to raise money in a unique way.*
>
> *Our goal is to raise $_____ as a way to _____(reason why). My personal goal is to sell _____ items and I was hoping I could count on you.*
>
> *I believe you will be interested in what we've developed for our community. Take a look at the information on this flyer and help us out if you can. I'm certain you can find something to your liking and which might be beneficial to you.*
>
> *(Closing) Thanks a lot for your support and have a great day."*

4. Be sure your members know when they hand a flyer to each person, they challenge the potential customer to help them reach their personal goal. After encouraging their participation, be sure to thank them for their consideration and support. Unless the Supporter places an immediate order, plan to get the order and payment later by checking back with them, because they will be expecting you to do so. It's simply a follow-up courtesy offered to them.

5. Have more flyers, with sales order forms on the back, available at your organization's home office or at your Fundraising Chair's home. That way, if a member runs out of flyers, more will be available. The Fundraising Chair should be sure to bring an additional supply of flyers to the next regular membership meeting.

6. Continue passing out flyers every two weeks for a few months. Evaluate whether you need to continue or pause your efforts for a couple of months and then continue.

7. At each meeting, as you are passing out more flyers to members, allow for testimonials on what they've achieved so far. Report these at the next event, meeting or in your newsletter. Also, refer to your Goal Thermometer you've been updating along the way.

**\* Email Blast \***

If you have an email list of your members and supporters, a quick way to get people interested in your fundraiser is to quickly send them a note by email asking them to join your fundraising efforts on a specified kick off date.

Initially, send a note to your members asking them to:

1.) Consider participating in your fundraising campaign as a Fundraising Team Member and help tell others about the group's fundraiser they are helping with.

2.) Prompt these same members to become their own first customer. After becoming a customer themselves, they can then send an email invitation (example below) to others, outside of the membership who they know (like their relatives, friends and neighbors), using the online Fundraising Website link given to your group by the fundraising company.  They may also use Twitter, Facebook, Pinterest, TotalSnap or Google+ to alert their friends to join them.

Action Guide

1. Get your Fundraising Committee on board. Compile the email addresses of all of your membership into one secure database you'll send emails to.

2. If you are offering incentives or prizes, for individual sales achievement by members, make arrangements to secure those items before your campaign begins. You'll see the sample email below is offering an incentive or prize item (which your group will supply) if each secures five people to buy *(Product Company Name here) products*.

You may not desire to offer an incentive, but realize it has been shown very effective to offer some type of bonus to improve fundraising sales. It could be: a pizza coupon, a $20 Wal-Mart Gift Card, a free bag of coffee, a free item you've secured through a local merchant, a restaurant gift certificate, etc. Your group provides the incentive as you deem appropriate. (*If you do not use an incentive, then please remove any indication of it in your email*).

3. Send a brief, introductory pre-announcement email to your membership indicating you will soon be conducting a "totally unique online fundraiser" and that you'll need their participation as a Fundraising Team Member. Place an article in your monthly newsletter if you have one. Provide an official kick off date so everyone knows when to be looking for the official email kickoff.

Here's a quick example of the pre-announcement email:

### *Major Announcement!*

*Our organization is officially announcing a phenomenal fundraiser which we will be implementing within the next two weeks. It's a totally unique online fundraiser which I believe you will be excited about. I will be asking for your careful consideration to assist me.*

*We are anticipating 100% participation from our members as the kick off occurs. I also believe it will be to your benefit to join us early on in this major effort to raise funds by being one of the first supporters.*

*Be on the lookout and get ready to join in the action!*

*Sincerely,*

*Charity CEO*

This pre-announcement can be sent each week for several weeks to build excitement and focus. Just change the words up somewhat each time.

You may want to use an audio-visual Email Messaging or Voice Mail Messaging Systems available online to alert your membership. These audio-visual messaging systems allow you to record and send real audio messages to your membership via email. You can also post a video on YouTube and embed the link in your email announcement.

4. On the scheduled kick off date, send the Kick Off email (*everything between the two dashed lines in the next 3 pages*) to your entire organization's membership or to your Fundraising Team Members if different. *This is not spam since they are already in your opt-in email list.* You as the Chair should *remove the portion italicized in (parenthesis) below* before sending.

You'll see a reference to *www.ProductCompanyName.com/yourgroupname* shown in the email. Most online product or service companies are now offering ways for their nonprofit groups and schools to provide their supporters with online ordering.

If there is no product website available, you may want to scan the fundraising flyer and order form and load it as a PDF document on your own group's website and give that website address in its place.

5. As the fundraiser unfolds, to see what actual activity is occurring, check in with your Fundraising Team Members by email. If any of your members have not ordered any product, you may want to call them and encourage them to do so. You are shooting for 100% participation from your membership first.

*Send this email first to your Fundraising Team Members:*

▪▪▪▪▪▪▪▪▪▪▪▪▪▪▪▪▪▪▪▪▪▪▪▪▪▪▪▪▪▪▪▪▪▪▪▪▪▪▪▪▪▪▪▪▪▪▪▪▪▪▪▪▪▪▪▪▪▪▪▪▪▪

Dear **Jane TeamMember:**

It's time to officially launch our organization's *(Product Name here)* Fundraising Campaign by email and your participation is the key to our success! We are anticipating 100% participation from all of our Members with this Fundraising Campaign.

Here's how you can help by completing Steps One and Two below:

**Step One – Read And Complete Instruction Items 1 – 6**

1. First, become familiar with the *(Product Name here)* Fundraising Website www.ProductCompanyName.com/*yourgroupname* (*replace this fictitious website with the real one given by your online product/ service company or with your online PDF document*) by buying your own items. This is important, because we are aiming for a 100% Participation Goal.

2. For effectiveness, you should become a Customer first. You could easily be asked by any Supporter you contact, "Are you participating in the fundraiser?" It is best if you can answer "yes" to that question without hesitation.

3. Send the sample email below (**Step Two**) to your family, neighbours and friends who are not members of our organization and ask them to help us raise funds. You may consider posting it on Facebook or other social media as well. In support of our organization, invite them to buy from our Fundraising Product Website.

4. As a special appreciation for helping us reach our goal, our organization is offering a (*list item here*) to all Fundraising Team Members who have at least 5 customers purchasing products through their efforts.

5. The more emails you send (like the one in Step Two), the more funds and financial support we will raise for our organization!

6. Finally, your friends and family can also participate in our fundraising campaign when they send the same email (Step Two) to their friends and family.  So please encourage them to do it on your behalf.

I look forward to seeing your participation with all of us.

Sincerely,

John TeamLeader

Fundraising Chair



**Step Two –Email Sent To Friends And Family**

*As a Fundraising Team Member here's the basic email of what you'll send to your friends and family. Touch it up a little to personalize it if you wish.*


Hi _____:

I wanted to be the first to let you know that *(my organization)* has just kicked off its online fundraising campaign where I'm serving as one of the Fundraising Team Members.

We've found a new way to raise money for our group this year. **It's fast and easy for you to help too.**  I need at least 5 people who will help me reach my goal and I was hoping you would agree to be one of them.

Please go to our group's website www.ProductCompanyName.com/yourgroupname and see what we have to offer.  Simply choose one or more of the products we are selling and help us raise funds.

These funds will be used for _____.

Basically, when you buy _____ from our Fundraising Product Website, it helps our organization raise funds through a portion of the sale.

Just go here…  www.ProductCompanyName.com/yourgroupname to view our website and help me reach my fundraising goal!

Thanks _____ (*the Supporter's Name*) for your interest and support.

Jane Helper

Fundraising Team Member
_____ (*My Organization*)


P.S. Help us reach our financial goal faster when you forward this message straight to other people you know. After ordering your products, you simply email a similar introduction to your friends and family just like I'm doing. Feel free to post the link with a brief note on your Facebook, Pinterest or social media page too. It will surely help me! Thanks!

••••••••••••••••••••••••••••••••••••••••••••••••••••••••••••••••


## * Event Survey Handouts *


Attend any event you are associated with and ask the attendees to take a brief survey which you are conducting. At the end of the survey ask them to consider helping your organization. As they depart, hand them a copy of your product sales flyer and a way to mail in their order or the way to go online to your group's Fundraising Website and buy some items.

Such events to consider include, Festivals, Dinners, Crafts Fair, Picnics or BBQ's, Concerts, Plays, Fashion Shows, Food Seminars, Talent Shows, Cooking Contests, Services, Home Shows, Health Fairs, Building Dedication, Parades, Dances, Amusements, Auctions, Bazaars, Contests/Games, Flea Markets or similar.

If you have a fair or event in your local community, then you may want to secure a booth and highlight your nonprofit efforts by handing out flyers, holding a brief seminar, and signing up people for a FREE Drawing. The free drawing is designed to purposefully gather names, phone, and email addresses of people you can contact later and get involved with your fundraiser.

Action Guide

1. Begin by investigating local events.  Later as you master the local show schedules, you may spread out to other parts of your geographical region.  Compile your list by the date of the event; along with, locations, registration fees and contact persons.

2. With your Fundraising Committee's help, rank each according to the desire for your members to be able to attend and participate in the "fun factor".  You should definitely plan to have fun, because your positive attitude will certainly spill over to the crowd as you talk about your nonprofit organization's fundraiser.

3. Make sure each Survey Team Member is also a supporter, because they will be asked by the prospective customer, "Are you participating in the fundraiser?"  It is good when an affirmative answer is given in response.

4.  Create a small, brief 3 – 5 question survey form about 1/4 page size (see sample below).   Change the questions to what you think would apply to your organization or geographic area.  Please avoid political or controversial questions.

5.  Prepare to attend the event by getting your product sales flyers and blank survey forms printed and ready.

The contact information given to you on the form will also help you locate the winner of the prize you are offering.

On the form you will ask for their phone number, address, and email address.  State clearly that you will not share, rent or sell their name to anyone else.

You can then use this information to market your fundraising products.  This gives you a good pool of prospects to email your fundraising website address to or mail a copy of your fundraising flyer and how they can help.

6.  Secure the prizes (either donated or bought) you'll be offering if people fill out the small survey card.  It might be a Gift Basket with various products you are offering in your fundraising brochure or anything of value.

Display prizes at the event to draw even more attention to what you are offering with your fundraiser.  Also, prominently display any fundraising products you'll be offering at your event booth table.

7. A few times during the day, at the event, you might want to conduct a "10 Minute Overview" about your organization and your fundraiser.

8. Follow up with a "courtesy call" or email to everyone who filled out the "Survey – Prize Drawing" Form. Thank them for their participation, share the results of the survey, and ask them if you can add them to your email or newsletter for updates about your efforts.

---

**Survey – Prize Drawing Form**

1. What is your favorite nonprofit group in our area? _____

2. What do you like most about them?
_____

3. What are ways that you support nonprofit groups in our area? _____

4. What charities do you feel are needed more? _____

5. What is the most efficient charity in our area? _____

Name_____

Phone _____

Email _____

Address _____

City/Zip _____

***Thanks for your participation.***
*Your Name will be placed in a drawing. Winners will be notified by email or phone. Your name will not be shared or sold.*

---

**\* Walk-A-Thon \***

Probably one of the most common fundraisers of all time is the Walk-A-Thon fundraiser. It is great for quickly instilling excitement and achieving solid fundraising results.

You'll find many organizations have utilized this proven fundraising technique to quickly draw in large numbers of new supporters and volunteers. Some of these groups include American Cancer Society, March of Dimes, American Heart Association, American Lung Association, and National Right To Life among others.

Each walk participant who signs up to be a "walker" will first be asked to become a customer themselves and buy one of the products, because they will be asked by their sponsors, "Are you participating in the fundraiser?" It is good for them to answer "yes" to the question.

You offer as a part of the Walk-A-Thon, a "participation thank you gift" given to each sponsor for their sponsorship at a certain dollar level. This "thank you gift" will be one of the product items they can choose from your fundraising brochure. This item will be paid for out of their financial sponsorship.

Each walk participant (a member of your organization) will ask their friends and neighbors to become one of their sponsors. Sponsorships, in this instance, do not qualify as "tax exempt" donations.


For becoming a...

**Walk Sponsor** - ask for a $15.00 donation and then plan to give them a choice of any single item from your fundraising sales brochure or flyer...

- A small 7 oz. candle scent of their selection.
- A 10oz. bag of gourmet coffee of their flavor selection.
- A tub of cookie dough of their selection.

**Event Sponsor** - ask for a $30.00 donation and then plan to give them a choice of...

- Three small 7 oz. candle scents of their selection.
- Two 10oz. bags of gourmet coffee of their flavor selection.
- Two tubs of cookie dough of their selection.


These are examples only, but you can get with your fundraising distributor or chosen product company and offer practically any item that does not cost much to purchase.  Remember, the money made between the sponsorship level and the cost of the item is pure profit.

The 'Walk Participant' should always ask for the sponsorship money upfront before the walk takes place (monies and walk forms will be turned in to the Fundraising Chair or Registration Coordinator by the Walk Participant before the Walk-A-Thon occurs).  It's not about how many miles they walk, but about sponsoring their attendance at the event so there should be no worries about getting the sponsoring funds upfront.

It is not advisable to offer these sponsorships as donations for a "Tax Deduction" according to IRS rules, because the Sponsor is receiving something of value for their support.  See the **Tax Issues** section for more detail for receiving something of value vs. token items of thanks.

After the event, your organization's Fundraising Campaign Chair will buy enough items to settle all sponsorship choices.  The items from all Sponsors will be consolidated and purchased from the fundraising company at the conclusion of the Walk-A-Thon money turn in date which is usually at the event itself.

If the turn-in date is before the event, then the items may actually be ready at the walk for Walk Participants to pick up after the Walk-A-Thon and then distribute to their Sponsors later that day or in the week.

Once these items have been purchased and delivered from the product company, distribution occurs back through the walk participants who will in turn, deliver the items to their Walk-A-Thon Sponsor.

When Walk Participants bring the products to the Sponsors, a **Thank You' Instruction Use Card** (see below) and a product flyer are delivered.  The 'Thank You' Instruction Use Cards can be printed ten to a page with a business card or shipping label template from Microsoft Word at http://office.microsoft.com/en-us/templates/

This allows the Sponsor to further help the group by mailing in an additional order (from family and friends) or going to the group's fundraising website and ordering more products if they like.

Action Guide

1. Secure the location for a starting gate.  This could be in a quiet neighborhood with little traffic on the street, inside a gymnasium, neighborhood park, enclosed mall, school track field, large parking lot or other area.  It doesn't have to be a long Walk-A-Thon, because a few miles will work perfectly.

2.  Recruit a Route Coordinator.  This person will contact the police and city officials and complete the proper permits, recruit members to help manage the route, secure traffic cones and tape to mark the route.  Secure orange vests for all volunteers along the route (most sheriff and county road departments have these).  Make sure every worker has a cell phone with instructions to call 911 in case of emergencies.

3. Recruit several judges who maintain the integrity of the walk.  This is more important if you have a race which extends 5 miles or more and you offer prizes for the top finishers.  Judges must be located at intervals and should record those who come through their checkpoint.  It is helpful if you have numbered tags attached to each walk participant to help identify them.

4. Set up a well-planned Home Base site that will handle large amounts of walkers or racers. Perhaps have your Walk-A-Thon at a mall with your own sign-up table right inside the event. Set up tables and chairs for the walkers to use after the race. You may want to provide a small stage if you plan to make announcements of winners and prize recipients. Provide a pleasant atmosphere as people gather before the walk with music, musicians playing or a carnival like atmosphere complete with clowns, etc. (or choose your own simple theme).

5. Have a person in charge of Public Relations. This person will have the responsibility to get the word out well in advance of the walk. He or she will notify the chamber of commerce, civic organizations, TV and radio, and write press releases for the newspaper and online news outlets. This person should provide certificates of recognition to all volunteers who have helped as coordinators or assisted in the planning and implementation. The Public Relations Coordinator should make sure any dignitaries in attendance are properly recognized.

6. Recruit a Prize Coordinator. This person is responsible for locating simple door prizes, awards, and certificates. If needed, they should ask local or national businesses for door prizes and gifts. An appropriate set of prizes could be special 'Gift Baskets' which you've packed with the various products you're offering. This person also sets and secures the awards for Sponsorship Levels achieved by Walk Participants.

7. Secure someone to handle registration. The Registration Coordinator is responsible for properly recording all participants as they enter. This person works with the Prize Coordinator to properly recognize those who should receive door prizes and other awards for Sponsorship Level achievements. The Registration Coordinator collects any monies and Walk-A-Thon Sponsor Sign-Up Forms (see example in the **Tools And Forms** section). This coordinator reports back to the Fundraising Committee and members on the amount of participation and total money raised. Four weeks before the event, the Registration Coordinator sends out a letter to all members with a Walk-A-Thon Sponsor Sign-Up Form or the Product Sales Form you will be using to gather Sponsors. Make sure all Fundraising Committee members and board members participating know they are expected to gather Sponsors too. These leaders should set the pace and be the first to have a Sponsorship form (or product sales flyer) filled up.

8. All Coordinators responsible should meet weekly to coordinate all preparations. Two weeks after the initial announcement letter, all Walk

Participants (volunteer walkers) should be contacted by mail and reminded about the event and the fact you are expecting to see them in attendance. Challenge them to gather as many Sponsors as they can get. If your Walk Participants have an e-mail address, Twitter account or social media page (Facebook, Pinterest); you may wish to use it to update them each week after the initial announcement. There should be words of encouragement from the President or Key Leader of your organization and any final instructions right before attending the actual event.

9. At the Walk-A-Thon, staff (Coordinators and their helpers) should be wearing matching shirts with a label on their shirts showing they are a part of your organization's Walk-A-Thon. All staff should keep everything upbeat. Be sure to have a lot of things happening at the event with plenty of announcements. Display the various Fundraising Products, Brochures, door prizes and/or awards at the registration area. Have your registration tables clearly marked and staffed. Be sure to have plenty of cash to make change if someone new (not yet sponsored) arrives and wants to participate in the walk. You may also want to have a laptop to connect with the internet (from a nearby WI-FI or Hotspot) to receive credit card payments. Also offer some select brochure items to the top winners of your Walk-A-Thon fundraiser as an incentive that your group is providing. Have a good time.

10. After the event, make sure the total amount raised is reported to all your participants and your members. Order enough products to fulfill your Sponsor commitments. Have each walk participant deliver the appropriate items directly to their Sponsors. Include a label with each product delivered showing instructions on how to get more products from your group's Fundraising Product Website or how to mail in an order. Use the 'Thank You' Instruction Use Card shown in this section. You may elect to include a copy of the brochure when you deliver your items for them to pass on to friends and neighbors (with the final date to turn in orders clearly marked).

*An Alternative* – Also offer at Marathons, Iron-Man Contests, Swimming Events or other events where the actual participants raising funds will be able to receive one of the fundraising products for achieving certain levels of Sponsorships. You may also want to have actual products for sale at these events too. Have the brochures and sales order forms available to take orders with cash or check made out to your group.

**\* Call-A-Thon Campaign \***

Calling a list of your members and supporters direct is one of the fastest ways to get the word out about your Fundraising Campaign. I've used Call-A-Thons effectively to close out my fundraising year and meet the goals.

There is a "calling script" in this section which you may adapt to your group's own personal narrative.

If you already have a website or blog where you have posted your Fundraising Website link or the URL where you've posted a PDF of your product sales flyer, simply tell those you call to go to your nonprofit group website and click on the fundraising program link for more details.

If you don't have a group website, it is suggested you obtain an easily read URL Web Address from a reputable Domain Name Registrar (i.e. Register.com, Hosting-Nation.com, godaddy.com, etc.) allowing you to link and redirect your Fundraising Product Website address through it. These domain names are usually less than $12/year. It will make pronouncing your Fundraising Website address easier over the telephone and is a simple way to direct your supporters to your Fundraising Products Website where they're displayed.

Action Guide

1. Recruit a calling team of at least 7 people. Calling Team Members may already be a part of your Fundraising Committee or you may need to recruit new volunteers just for this campaign. Make sure your Calling Team Members are themselves participating and have bought one or more products, because they will be asked by the prospective customer, "Are you participating in the fundraiser?" It is good if the answer is in the affirmative. Begin compiling your complete list of members and supporters whom you'll be calling.

2. If you haven't built a call database, then put this ever-growing list of contacts into an Address Book on your organization's computer. Perhaps use Outlook, ACT!, OpenOffice.org BASE, GoldMine, Outlook Express or other database manager.

3. Divide the names up among Calling Team Members. Ideally, you will want to have 10 – 20 names per Calling Team Member. If you don't have at least six Calling Team Members, you should decide to conduct the campaign using fewer team members with the calls spread out over several weeks so you'll not overload them all at once.

4. Secure the date and location for your campaign. You will need a bank of telephones (bank, company, church, etc.) or have team members use their own cell phones if they don't mind. The key is to have the calling campaign conducted at one main location to create excitement and keep the accounting in one location.

5. Create a script or use the one below and alter as you desire so that everyone will be on the same page as each practices it. Have team members speak conversationally rather than memorizing the suggested script.

6. Print off the contact names from your address book and separate into 10 – 20 names per Calling Team Member. Have everyone show up and begin calling. Display a goal chart for everyone to view. Make it fun and have a bell to ring (i.e. cowbell) every time someone gets an indication of an order. Make sure you make a note of each contact and their decision so that you can conduct a follow-up if necessary. Have snacks and drinks for all.


Sample Calling Script


*Hi _____, this is*
*_____ (your name) with _____*
*(your organization) and I wanted to be the first to let you know that our organization has just kicked off its fundraising product campaign where I'm serving as one of the Calling Team Members.*

*It's a totally unique fundraiser which I believe you will be excited about. We are expecting 100% participation from our members and I am asking for your careful consideration.*

*I've been asked to call at least 5 people to help me reach my goal, and I was hoping you would possibly agree to be one of those who could help me. Is that possible?*

*(Wait for a response)*

*Basically, we've decided to offer _____ products to help our group raise funds and gather supporters. And when you buy any of the products from our fundraising flyer or Fundraising Product Website, it helps our organization raise funds through a portion of the sale.*

*We plan to use the funds to _____.*

*Do you have a pencil to write down our Fundraising Product Website? (Wait until they do.) Just go here – http://ProductCompanyName.com/yourgroupname to view our website or product flyer and help our organization reach its fundraising goal.*

*I've already selected my products, so we're already on our way to a successful fundraiser. I hope that I can count on your participation with us too? I'll certainly follow up with you to make sure there were no problems in choosing a product and to answer any other questions you may have. Thanks again for your consideration.*

*Have a great evening.*

Alternative – If your group does not have a large list of your own members or supporters to contact, then an alternative calling campaign could be conducted to non-members who live in your community.

Conduct some investigation on consumer lists of people in your community from a reputable direct mail or list company.

Here are a few reputable list brokers or agencies available:

   All-n-One List Marketing - Allinonelistmarketing.com - 703-717-5621

   American List Council - alcdata.com - 609-580-2800

   Atlantic List Company - atlanticlist.com - 702-528-7482

   DirectMail.com - 866-284-5816

   DMG Direct, Inc. - dirmarketing.com - 888-282-2122

   InfoGroup (Direct Media Millard) – dmminfo.com - 202-973-5404 infoUSA.com - infousa.com - 800-555-5999

RMI Direct Marketing - rmidirect.com – 203- 825-4636

USA Data - usadata.com - 800-395-7707

Worldata.com - 800-331-8102


These lists will cost around $100 per 1,000 names so be careful and plan ahead.  These people may be on the FCC "Do Not Call" list, but this list does not specifically apply to nonprofit organizations seeking support.


Here's a sample call script for contacting new potential supporters.


*Hi, I'm calling for _____ (Prospect's name),*

*Hi _____ (Prospect's name), this is _____ (Your first and last name) with _____ (Your Organization).*

*How are you doing?  Great!*

*_____ (Prospect's name), I am part of a team calling our community and informing them about a new fundraising emphasis we're starting.  Everyone is excited about this new fundraiser and we want to give members of our community the opportunity to participate with us.*

*We plan to use the funds to _____.*

*Our fundraising program was carefully chosen to keep our community in mind, so we're getting the word out as quickly as possible.*

*Allow me to point you to our website for more information.  Please get a pencil and jot down this web address.   It would be - http://ProductCompanyName.com/yourgroupname where you can view our website or product flyer and help our organization reach its fundraising goal. As a courtesy to you I could also send this information to your email address for you.  Would like me to do that?  (If yes, then write down their email address and send the link immediately).*

*After you've reviewed our Fundraising Program, you can participate by simply buying one or more of the products offered.*

*I have already signed on board myself and am excited about what is being offered. I'm certain any one of the products will benefit you as well and I appreciate your consideration in helping us reach 100% of our fundraising goal.*

*I'll get that website link right over to you and I'll look forward to talking with you again soon. Thank you. Good bye.*

(Note: Avoid going into too much detail about the products – if asked simply explain, "That's the beauty of it! It's all explained online so we don't have to be experts!") If you have the Fundraising Product Website link or product flyer posted on your group's own website, then just send the person to your nonprofit group's website. Keep their name and phone number allowing you to follow up with a courtesy call and answer any questions they may have.

Voicemail / Answering Machine script while contacting new potential community supporters:

*"Hi, my name is _____ (Your Name) with*
*_____ (Your Nonprofit Organization) calling for*
*_____ (Prospect's first and last name).*

*I am part of a team calling you and other members of our community and informing them about a new product fundraising emphasis our organization has started.*

*I know every one of us is excited about this new product fundraiser and we wanted to call and give everyone in our community the opportunity to join us in this effort. I am hoping we'll reach 100% of our goal with your help.*

*Please take a moment and go to our fundraising website www.ProductCompanyName.com/yourgroupname or call back and give me your email address and I will be happy to forward the website link to you. I'll call back to go over this with you or feel free to call me anytime at ( _____ ) _____-_____ when you are able and I'll explain more. Thank you for your thoughtful consideration. Good bye."*

*An Alternative* – Secure a calling service or a predictive dialer service like phoneburner.com which may be more cost effective, especially if you do not have a lot of volunteers to conduct your own calling campaign. Use any search engine and type in key words like "calling services", "dialing services", "robocalls", "automated phone services" or "live operators" for other services available. Nonprofits are exempt from telemarketing call rules.

## * Gathering Of Friends *

Not everyone is comfortable asking for money or fundraising in a face-to-face situation. Instead of meeting with someone alone, what if you could invite several friends (members and supporters) to meet you in a comfortable, relaxed setting, drinking coffee, and where you share with them your fundraising product brochure? It would make it easier right?

The idea behind the Gathering Of Friends campaign is that everyone will be involved in helping you succeed at your event. And as people begin to join in, it will become contagious by allowing everyone the opportunity participate in reaching the 100% participation goal.

Action Guide

1. Begin by dividing your member and supporter list into groups of 7 – 10 invitees. Recruit a Host Team Member (this is your Fundraising Team Member) who will contact the invitees from each group to a 'gathering' typically at their home. See calling scripts located in this book for help in crafting an invitation call.

2. Perhaps instead of inviting only your members and supporters as invitees, why not also invite a few individuals from outside of your group membership? Perhaps you could concentrate on friends, neighbors and relatives who are not a part of your organization. On a pad of paper, create for yourself a "Potential New Customer List" to help you write down names of potential guests. This strategy is especially helpful if you do not have many supporters or members belonging to your group (i.e. a new nonprofit, a small church, a small club or fraternity, etc.). This could be people you do business with

(dentist, doctor, pharmacist, insurance agent, plumber, child's sports coach, co-worker, etc.)

3. Make sure each Host Team Member has already become a Customer, because they will be asked by their guests, "Are you participating in the fundraiser?" They will certainly want to say "yes" to the question.

4. Each Host Team Member should invite no more than 12 people (invitees from list and others like family and friends) to an informal gathering at their home or favorite setting without any interruptions expected. They should have coffee, tea, water and some treats to offer the guests. Each Host Team Member should call their guests the day before with a reminder of the gathering place and time.

5. The agenda at the gathering may look something like this:

- Set up your presentation area of your home. Have available a fundraising brochure (or product sales flyer) for each person to review. If you have a Fundraising Product Website from your chosen fundraising company then you may also have a computer running and opened to your Fundraising Website. Use a HDMI cable to hook up to your TV from your laptop computer or tablet to show everyone.
- Greet guests as they arrive.
- Serve tea, coffee, drinks, snacks, etc.
- Introductions -- ask each person to tell a little about something about their involvement with your nonprofit or a charity that they are involved with at the present. As an ice breaker, ask each one to tell of a particular experience when they were involved with your organization. It could be funny or sad as long as it involved them personally.
- Discuss a little about why you are involved with your nonprofit organization (or school) and why this gathering has been organized to share information and gather financial support through a unique product fundraiser as seen in the fundraising brochure or flyer.
- Show any video or pictures of a recent event of your organization if available. Mention why you are raising money and how reaching your financial goal will help. Ask if there are any questions. Answer them to the best of your ability.
- At this point, some hosts might feel comfortable giving away a door prize if your organization has secured one. Also make known that for 3 referrals (friends and family not present), who end up buying a product, they'll receive a free product (your group decides if they want to offer

incentives to guests from the brochure supplied by the fundraising company).

- Give each participant a "take home flyer" with more information about the products, the Fundraising Product Website address, contact information and the incentives plan for everyone.

- If you have a "thermometer goal chart" you can illustrate where your participation goal is at currently. Stress how you are aiming for 100% participation from your invited guests and their help will be especially appreciated to assist in reaching the goal.

- You should mention that as the host, you have also become a customer and will want to highlight what you've selected from the brochure. Point to the Thermometer Goal Chart and proceed to mark off with a red marker your involvement. If you have a co-chair then you should allow them to place their mark next, showing their participation as well. For instance, if you have ten guests, then each of you will mark off about 10% on the thermometer.

- Explain how to use the Sales Order Form and who to make their checks payable to. Once they have purchased their products and paid (don't accept COD), encourage them to go make their mark of participation on the Thermometer Goal Chart (have the red marker available and let them do the honor themselves).

- After everyone has had a chance to purchase products, review the Thermometer Goal Chart with everyone. Give a big "Hooray!" if you've reached 100% participation.

- Remind all about the "take home flyer" they can show to their friends and neighbors who can look over the products too. This will typically be a photocopy of the brochure and a simple sales order form which shows who they need to contact to place an order. Of course if you have a Fundraising Product Website, then their referral prospects can just place their order online.

- Close the gathering. Thank each for coming and restate how important their participation is valued. As a courtesy, let them know you plan to follow up with each of them and report the results of the group's efforts to reach their goal.

6. In your follow up to those who purchased products at your gathering, it is suggested that you mail a 'thank you' note to each for attending.

7. For those who did not purchase a product for some reason, send a note of appreciation for their attendance. Include a copy of the Thermometer Goal

Chart showing where you are currently at and further stress their consideration in achieving your 100% participation goal.

Emphasize the urgency of wrapping up your campaign and how you will follow up with them by phone in a timely manner. Also, include a small card with your nonprofit group's Fundraising Product Website if you've been given one, reminding them that they still have time to participate and make a difference.

Here is a checklist for success:

- Be cheerful, friendly, and enthusiastic when hosting your event.
- Remember, you are not "begging" for money, but merely giving your guests the opportunity to help your organization in a rather unique fashion... by buying one of your fundraising products.
- Take the time to generate interest and excitement at your event. Do not use high pressured sales tactics, yet stress your desire to reach the 100% participation goal.
- You are your own best supporter. You must purchase one or more products first before asking others to help out. *"Let he who would be moved to convince others, be first moved to convince himself".* [Thomas Carlyle]
- Use testimonials whenever you can. It gives credibility about how the products have been used by others.
- It's best to work in teams of two. The hosts, whether it is a husband/wife approach or two friends at the same organization can offer each other some comfort and moral support. Different roles may be used where one takes the social angle, building rapport, while the other is the knowledgeable expert answering questions about products.

**\* Peddler's Cart \***

Unlike the peddler's cart of past centuries which went from town to town, you will want to choose a single site for your cart where you sell the products.

Operating at a particular location, over a period of time, is the key to consistently raising money every day over a period of several weeks.

The Peddler's Cart is for small to medium sized groups wanting to make a big impact, draw a lot of attention to their cause, and use very little volunteer effort to work the cart.

Many malls offer kiosks or peddler's carts for rent or will allow you to set up your own. As a nonprofit organization you may be allowed by the management to set up your kiosk for free. It never hurts to ask and they may get some good publicity out of it. Also, consider mega-stores and department stores to provide some free space.

Don't forget that many mega-churches have a "mall" area where they serve coffee, refreshments and can easily allow some space for your effort, especially if it goes toward helping a ministry effort.

Your group will want to consider the holiday times where people tend to buy gifts like October, November, December, and February.

Action Guide

1. Begin by securing some display items for sale from your selected fundraising company or distributor. Let your distributor know what you are doing and why this first order will be small and will be used for displaying the products you'll be offering. If you are selling items like candles, you will want to get one of each scent and size offered. For food items like cookie dough, you will want to show the tub container only. Perhaps you've baked the cookies inside and offer one to each new customer as a free thank you surprise.

2. Secure your volunteer Sales Force. Make sure all Sales Force Members are participating and have become a Customer first, because they will surely be asked by any prospective customer, "Which product did you buy?" It is suggested you also have one new worker available at your cart for every two hours of operation. Rotate as your volunteer numbers dictate.

3. Stock your cart with all of the great selections showing the suggested retail pricing. You may also have "sales signs" posted if you want to offer any "specials".

4. Choose a set time to start your Peddler's Cart sales. The best times for a lot of traffic are usually around Thanksgiving and Christmas, but other sales days are great too like Independence Day and in February for Valentine's Day.

5. At the point of sale, offer payment by credit cards easily with a smart phone and a card reader from Square.com, PayPal or Intuit (all free). You will need to collect local and state taxes unless you are accepting donations and then giving item(s) away for a specific donation amount. Be sure to get with your local taxing authority and complete the necessary forms.

6. If anybody prefers to go home and place an order, then hand them a photocopy of your brochure with an accompanying sales order form showing where to mail it back to. You may also highlight your Fundraising Product Website address if you have one. You may even want to simply get their name and offer to give them a "courtesy call" and sell them a product later.

7. For those who do not want to take the time to stop and buy, have a generic "take home flyer" available to pass out to these mall shoppers as they pass by. If this is done, it would be a good idea to have a second person passing out the flyers while another is standing by to take orders.

*An Alternative* – Instead of "selling" items, try accepting suggested donations for specific item(s) you are offering. For example, for a donation of $10 or more give the new supporter a Discount Merchant Card (Pizza Card, Sandwich Card, etc.) as a "thank you" for their donation. Be sure to get their contact information for "a free product drawing" you'll automatically enter them in (This is up to you to decide and not the fundraising company you're buying from). Congratulations, you've just created an ongoing list of new prospects.

**\* Letter Campaign To Close Relatives Or Friends \***

A letter campaign to close relatives or friends should only be used by members for contacting to those they personally know very well. Most aunts, uncles, grandparents, and close family friends of members will be happy to support your efforts.

This option is simple, yet very effective for individuals and small groups. For larger groups, sending to former supporters, it would be better using a letter coming from a local (or national) celebrity to get the full affect.

Make the letter brief, but intriguing. Get right to the point on how much you are trying to raise, what the funds will be used for, and any other reason why you are asking for their support. Put yourself in your reader's shoes and imagine how you would like to receive a special offer to purchase items in support of your organization's effort.

If you suspect that many of your contacts will be past supporters, be sure to thank them for their past support and highlight what successes have been achieved through their support.

Be sure to personally sign your letter so those you contact will know that a real person is making this request and that this is not a form letter casually sent out by your organization.

In each personalized letter, try using some of the most powerful words in the English language as applicable. My favorites are shown here:

| | | |
|---|---|---|
| Absolutely | Exciting | Help |
| Amazing | Fantastic | Huge |
| Bargain | Free | Insider |
| Big | Friendly | Interesting |
| Buy | Gain | Kind |
| Caring | Genuine | Largest |
| Complete | Get | Latest |
| Confidential | Gift | Love |
| Discovery | Gigantic | Magic |
| Early | Greatest | Miracle |
| Easy | Guarantee | Money |
| Excellent | Health | New |

| | | |
|---|---|---|
| • Outstanding | • Reliable | • Tested |
| • Own | • Remarkable | • Thanks |
| • Partnership | • Reveal | • Thank You |
| • Phenomenal | • Results | • Tremendous |
| • Popular | • Revolutionary | • Unconditional |
| • Powerful | • Safety | • Unlimited |
| • Practical | • Save | • Useful |
| • Professional | • Secrets | • Valuable |
| • Profitable | • Sensation | • Wealth |
| • Proven | • Special | • Wonderful |
| • Purchase | • Successful | • You |
| • Quality | • Superior | • Your |
| • Receive | • Surprise | • Zest |
| • Reduced | • Terrific | |

These words come from a variety of sources over the years, so there is no one particular source to give credit to. You will find these words in many copy writing courses or imbedded in top fundraising sales letters, because they are powerful words which work very well. Use in a conversational tone and not one that's contrived.

Action Guide

1. Instruct individual Team Members to make a list and write down names and addresses of people they personally know outside of your membership.

Gather as many names of close friends, family, co-workers, vendors, business services they use, and congregation members who could support your efforts. It doesn't have to be a large list, but there should be a dozen or more for each Team Member.

2. Each individual member should write a personal letter making the case for what you hope to accomplish this year at your nonprofit organization and why he/she, as one of the members, is asking for their help.

Send your appeal letter out with a photocopy of the brochure. I emphasize photocopying the brochure, because the glossy brochures or flyers, typically provided free by a fundraising company, costs 25 cents or more apiece and they will not want to provide that many glossy brochures to include in each letter. Usually you will receive one glossy brochure per Fundraising Team Member at no cost.

3. There is a sample letter at the end of this book titled **Fundraising Introductory Letter From Nonprofit Members To Friends** which you might want to use and send out as a reference so that your Team Members can adapt it to their own personality.

If you have one, be sure to include your group's Fundraising Product Website address for them to review the products you are selling online.

Make sure you emphasize you'll be following up with each prospect personally if you do not hear from them within two weeks of your letter request. This will make them more inclined to take action before you call them.

4. Follow up by telephone to each who personally received a letter. Hearing an actual human voice may be the key to seal the product sale. Be polite and inquire whether they received your letter which was sent to them.

Ask if they have any questions and wish to purchase one or more of the products to help support your organization. Which product are they interested in?

Stress that your personal goal is to secure at least 5 customers and ask if you can mark them down as one of your new customers?

Offer them the proper mailing instructions for sending in their payment or for paying online. You may also offer to pick up their sales order form and payment at their discretion.

5. Finally, send out a letter of gratitude to all new Customers. Give them a report on the money you've raised to date.

Send out notices periodically as needed when new products arrive or any beneficial information occurs.

**\* Parent Meeting Kick Off \***

At the beginning of sports season or the school year there is usually a Parents Meeting for everyone to get acquainted. For this discussion, let's assume this as a school type parent's function, but you will want to adapt it to your particular group. Your group will certainly be different with an "end of year" emphasis versus a "first of the year" meeting instead.

At some point during the meeting, the object will be to inform parents or new members about what your organization needs and why you need to raise funds to accomplish the plans you are making. Do not try to "sell" them too hard on the products at this particular meeting.

You simply remark about how your chosen fundraiser will be offered to others in your community, but you want to share it with your parents first. Mention how you will be sending out a notice by: a.) flyer, b.) email, or c.) calling campaign in an attempt to get all parents on board quickly. Stress a 100% Participation Goal that you'll expect from them. That's it.

Don't go into too much detail during the first promotion meeting. If you have a social media page (i.e. Facebook, Pinterest), Microsite (TotalSnap.com), blog or group website, then state you'll post a link there directing them to your Fundraising Product Website where everyone can review the products.

Action Guide

1. At the meeting, have your Fundraising Chair give a brief overview of what you hope to accomplish with this unique fundraiser. Make sure the Chair and Key Leadership Team (President, Treasurer, Secretary, etc.) have each signed up as a Customer, because they will be asked by the new members, "Are you participating in the fundraiser?" The answer should be in the affirmative.

2. For entire schools where no Parent's Meeting occurs, you will send home a "Parent's Letter" via students (or email to parents) explaining the program and what you expect from your students. There is a form at the end of this book entitled "**Key Leader's Kickoff Letter**". Be sure to personalize the letter for

your particular organization and have someone else review it before printing and sending home with students for parents to read.

3. Always stress 100% participation. Whether your group actually achieves 100% participation by its members is beside the point. Place a "thermometer goal chart" in a prominent place at the meeting if you want to set a participation goal.

4. Have a display of sample products you will be selling which you've ordered ahead of time.

5. Take a few moments to recruit a few more Fundraising Committee Members from your parents during the first meeting or in follow-up recruitment calls.

6. Plan your first regular Fundraising Committee Member meeting (follow up meetings should be held monthly at a minimum). The first fundraising committee meeting might be a little more comfortable if held at a person's home.

7. Go over your fundraising agenda and discuss upcoming fundraising plans. Perhaps use the Year Long Comprehensive Fundraising Plan as a complete game plan for your entire annual fundraising program.

8. After the meeting, thank the new Fundraising Committee Members for coming and give each one a product brochure. Ask each to go ahead and choose one or more items and have it ready at the next meeting.

Stress how the Fundraising Committee Members are expected to "lead by example" and purchase their products before they reach out to other members and the community. The goal is 100% participation from all leaders. This is a marvelous tool (100% Leader Participation) to show the community how you are so excited about this particular product fundraiser that 100% of your Key Leaders are on board too.

9. At the next group, team or parent meeting announce the kickoff date of your product fundraising campaign. If you will be giving incentive prizes away, offer the best ones to the first 10 families who order products or for all who order products before they leave.

You will get many that order something that that night. Congratulations, you are already achieving success.

Give them something special for these "early birds" and then provide different prizes to others signing up later if you wish. You will be glad you offered prizes to the first sign ups, because even 10 families will start to multiply the funding for your group in a big way.

*Here's a Success Tip!* You might want to recruit those first 10 or more families who participate earlier as your Campaign Team Leaders, because they've proven to be real "go getters".

10. Finally, implement the fundraising method you've chosen from this book and conduct your Fundraising Product Campaign. Stay focused on accomplishing your goal.

## * One-On-One Visitation Meetings *

Here is a model for any Fundraising Team Member wishing to personally approach a potential customer face-to-face and ask for their participation.

The Fundraising Team Member should:

- Have first signed up themselves as a customer by purchasing items on-the-spot, through a fundraising sales brochure or flyer, or through the organization's Fundraising Product Website if there is one.
- Be well informed about the organization's exact fundraising needs. Why are you raising money? How much will you need?
- Tell the supporter that they are personally participating and have already bought a product as a customer.
- Be knowledgeable about the products. Which products did they purchase and which one is most popular? Be organized in presenting the fundraising products to others. Show the product brochure and ask which products the customer would prefer to buy. Use the sales order form to record the selected purchase.
- Be able to make a report back to the Fundraising Campaign Chair or Fundraising Team Leader.

It would be advisable for the visiting Fundraising Team Member to call the prospective customer and make an appointment ahead of time.

Here's a sample call script for setting the appointment.

*"Hello, is _____ (Member's name) there?"*

*"Hi _____ (Member's name), this is _____ (Your first and last name) with _____ (Your organization).*

*How are you doing?  Great!  Have you been notified about our new fundraising program?  (wait for a response)*

*Well, I've been recruited to help contact a few of our members and past supporters this week to personally give the presentation about the program to them.  I was asked to give you a call and make an appointment to meet so that you too can see what we're so excited about.*

*Is that possible?  (they should respond in the affirmative)  Good!*

*What would be the best time to visit with you this week?  Anytime Tuesday or Thursday would be good for me.  OK, we'll meet _____ (date) at _____ (time) at _____ (place).  I'll see you there.  Good bye."*

Action Guide

1. The Fundraising Team Member prepares for their meeting.  This same Team Member should have already signed up as a Customer prior to the meeting.

2. The Fundraising Team Member meets with the prospect on time.

3. Show the Goal Thermometer Chart and stress, *"We are looking for 100% participation from all of our members and supporters.  I've already bought a product myself.  Can we count on you?"*

4. Show the fundraising product brochure and allow them to choose their product preferences.  Have some sales forms available to record their order.

Go ahead and receive their payment with the order (no COD;s) or make arrangements to come by again and pick it up.

5.  Send a note of gratefulness for the member's participation with your group's fundraising efforts.

Note:  If you belong to an organization with an online Fundraising Product Website which allows individuals to purchase products and have it shipped to their home, then you may still wish to meet members personally and show them how to go online and purchase products.

Sometimes in small organizations, that have just a few members, it may be desirable to assign a Fundraising Committee Member to personally reach out to each member for achieving 100% participation.  Just a few contacts each month by a Fundraising Committee Member promoting participation through the website, spread out over a few months, could be considerable.

**\* Year Long Comprehensive Fundraising Plan \***

This final fundraising campaign plan incorporates many of the various methods previously described into an ongoing fundraising promotion campaign that allows you to "hit the ground running" while being comprehensive enough as a fundraising program lasting throughout the year.

Basically, you will promote your fundraising program as much as you can and in as many ways as possible including through a Fundraising Product Website (*www.ProductCompanyName.com/yourgroupname)* if you have one. This type of comprehensive fundraising effort will be able to direct your supporters on how they can assist your organization from many different angles.

Simply follow the Action Guide in the timeframe you have allotted for your organization.  You can easily accomplish a good portion of this plan within a one to four week period with other helpers involved.

Make sure that you lock in each individual phase of your comprehensive campaign on an annual calendar as you can.  This simple action will go a long way to keeping everyone on track.

As you proceed through each step, be sure to add names with contact information to your growing contact management database. Building a list of supporters and potential prospects is a critical step to ongoing success, especially as you begin to follow up with everyone, give updates as they become necessary and thank them all for their participation.

Action Guide

1. Post your Fundraising Product Website link immediately on your own nonprofit group's main website (Homestead.com), blog or Microsite (TotalSnap.com). Post a banner if you can create one which draws attention to your goal and kickoff date. Post this link on all social media outlets like your organization's Facebook page, Pinterest page or by tweets (Twitter.com).

2. Your charity CEO, President, Board Chair and/or Executive Director should schedule appointments with every key leader in your organization using the **One-On-One Visitation Meetings** method or the **Gathering Of Friends** plan. Get a commitment from every Committee Chair and Board Member to buy one or more products. Have them place the group's Fundraising Product Website link on their own personal social media webpage, blog and as a part of their "signature" at the bottom of every email they send out.

3. Recruit a Fundraising Campaign Chair for a specific product campaign the first week. Make sure they agree to commit and actually buy one or more of the products. The Fundraising Campaign Chair should be involved in every aspect of the rest of this comprehensive plan.

4. Send out an email to all of your members immediately using the **Email Blast** method. Report in the email that every key leader is involved at the *100% Participation Level*. This is true because you've already approached the Key Leaders and secured their commitment and order.

5. Send out an announcement in your group's newsletter using the **Newsletter Announcements** marketing effort. Continue sending weekly updates, if possible and certainly send newsletters with product highlights and testimonials over the next few months. Use the thermometer goal chart to plainly show what is being accomplished. Announcements should include those key leaders who are already involved and report 100% participation by your decision making board.

6. At your next big membership meeting, use **The Gathering** method or the **Parent Meeting Kick Off** method to spread the word. Make sure you have plenty of product brochures, sales order forms and show some products for all in attendance to see. Have various key leaders, who have already used some of the products, give brief personal testimonials.

7. Send a letter to each of your members, top volunteers and key donors asking them to reach out to their friends. Use the **Letter Campaign To Close Relatives Or Friends** method for this.

8. Send an **Email Blast** to everyone in your growing database and/or compile a list of community supporters and ask them to promote your Fundraising Product Website to friends and family they know. In the email ask each to help you spread the word by posting links and comments to their own social media outlets. Perhaps even have links posted on your website to any videos you've placed on YouTube for people to see and hear from the actual people who are benefitting from your efforts.

9. Finally, wrap up contact to your members and supporters with a **Call-A-Thon Campaign.** This would be a great time to thank those who became a customer and remark about how you would appreciate if it they could pass the word to their friends and neighbors. If you then feel like you want to continue reaching out into your community even more, simply go ahead with **The Canvas Approach, Walk-A-Thon, Peddler's Cart** or **Event Survey Handouts** plan to gather more names and interest.

10. As with any fundraising campaign, 'Thank' everyone for their consideration and involvement over and over again in every correspondence. This will go a long way to getting them involved and staying connected as a satisfied supporter of your group.

# Additional Marketing Efforts

The contact list of your customers, prospects and supporters is like "Gold". Why keep a list of supporters (customers)? Obviously, it is to contact each one of them next year or anytime during the year. Don't assume customers from this year will automatically remember to contact your group next year and support you. You must be the one who reaches out to them instead.

One of the most important phases of any fundraising campaign is about Reaching Out beyond your own membership. Now that you've started your fundraiser and have conducted your fundraising effort internally to your membership, you will want to have your fundraising committee concentrate on reaching out to the community and telling them about what you are accomplishing.

You will find here some creative ways of introducing your fundraising products. These are just a few ideas to get you started.

## ➢ Conference Calls

Get your prospects to connect to a conference call you've set up. This is a great way to add some power to your prospecting efforts. It's also a method where members can bring their friends (prospective supporters) in to listen in on a candid discussion about your fundraising products and efforts to secure support.

To secure your own conference call capability, try some of the free programs available on the internet like TotallyFreeConferenceCalls.com, AnyMeeting.com, GlobalConference.com and FreeConference.com. There are many other programs out on the internet so be sure to do some research to find what will work best for your organization.

Also, online autoresponder software like GetResponse.com has the capability with their premium package to send video and audio by email so you might want to use it to send recorded calls to those who were not able to attend the conference call. To send audio presentations via email or posted in your website or blog try using GoldMail (PointAcross.com), techsmith.com, bombbomb.com, Slide Share (slideshare.net), and byoaudio.com which have good capabilities.

One final form of conference call can be done by video with applications from Skype (Skype.com click "Tools" then "Extras" for conferencing tools). I've seen increasing usage of Skype by younger people who want to connect with their friends face to face. Other options are Tokbox.com, MyVideoTalk.com, MegaMeeting.com, TeamViewer.com, Zoho.com, GoToMeeting.com, webex.com, iWowWe.com and Logitech Vid (LogiTech.com).

You can also show and explain the contents of a brochure much more easily by video calling. In today's increasingly busy world, this may be an option for smaller groups especially those connected by technology.

➤ **Radio Spot Announcement**

Radio spots work if you can get them promoted often enough by a commercial radio station (not a nonprofit radio station) which agrees to sponsor your ad or carry it as a Public Service Announcement. They may need to rephrase the sample spot shown below to fit within a 30 second or 1 minute segment spot.

It is recommended that you secure your own easily pronounced domain name web address which can be redirected to your actual Fundraising Product Website if you'll be offering one. It is easier to give an easily pronounced domain name over the air rather than trying to spell your original Fundraising Product Website address which may have too many letters verbalize effectively. You may purchase a domain name from a reputable online merchant (i.e. Register.com, hostgator.com, godaddy.com, Hosting-Nation.com, etc.) which will allow you to redirect your exact Fundraising Product Website address through it.

Here is a sample radio spot that might be used.

_____ (your nonprofit organization's name) is now offering

an easy way for our community supporters to help us raise funds for our

cause. That's right, it's now easier than ever to help us by purchasing one of *our preferred products online.  Go to www.YourBestFantasticFundraiser.com*

*(as an example only)    You'll get…*

- *A variety of product choices*
- *Fast shipping and delivery direct to your door*
- *Secure payment acceptance online.*

*Purchasing some of our products online has never been faster or easier.*

*Logon to www.YourBestFantasticFundraiser.com or call us for more details at (xxx) xxx – xxxx*

*That's www.YourBestFantasticFundraiser.com or (xxx) xxx – xxxx*

➤ **Newsletter Announcements**

Announcements made in your group's newsletter are an extremely effective way to educate everyone about your product fundraiser.  In many ways, it will become a continual marketing method of reminding everyone that you anticipate 100% participation from your group's members and community supporters.

You should be consistent and highlight the following each month in your organization's newsletter:

- Your Fundraising Product Website address – *www.ProductCompanyName.com/yourgroupname*.
- Product spotlight – highlight one of the products each month and any benefits that it provides.
- Have a testimonial from someone who has used one of the products.  Where practical, give personal testimonials of what others have purchased and why.
- Don't edit your message so much that you lose its emotional appeal.  It should be as personal as possible.
- Display the thermometer goal chart (reduced size) showing what participation level has been reached over the prior week (or month) since the last newsletter went out.

- Provide a note from the President or charity CEO stating, "Many of you continue to offer positive comments about our product fundraiser. I am pleased to announce the following who have become new customers this month." a.) Mr._____, b.) Ms._____, c.) Mrs._____ and d.) Ms._____ having all joined the rest of us toward our 100% participation goal. Thank you all for your support."

*Alternative:* Do the same as shown above with your eNewsletter sent by email if your organization has one.

> **Acquiring New Prospects**

From time to time you will need to add to your prospect list and give others an opportunity to participate in your next product fundraiser. Get with your fundraising committee and brainstorm ways to involve those in your community who are not a part of your current supporters or membership.

Here are a few ideas to start with:

**Booth At A County Fair or Flea Market**

Place a booth at your county fair which explains what your organization is all about. Offer a door prize or series of door prizes, when someone signs up for your "free newsletter" at your booth. Make sure you indicate that their name will be placed on the newsletter mailing list and it will not be sold or loaned to any other group or business. Allow them to receive their prize without being present to win. Be sure to get full name, address, phone number, e-mail address, and title (Mr., Mrs., Dr., Ms.).

**Send Survey Out To Members**

Send a survey form to your current members asking for suggestions on how to improve your organization. Include several spots on the form for referrals of 2 to 4 friends that might be interested in receiving information or news about your organization and fundraising efforts.  Be sure to update all new contact information to your database such as current address, phone, e-mail address, and interests when they come in.  When sending any information to the new prospects, be sure to mention that your organization was referred to them by one of your members and it's not a random mailing or spam email.


## Company Newsletters

Ask your current supporters who own businesses or are employed at large companies to include a small ad (information box) about your nonprofit group in their next company newsletter.  If you have a free service or items that you commonly offer new supporters, then offer it.  You may wish to provide a "coupon" type ad in the newsletter or offer a "Special Sale" on the products.  Include your group's Fundraising Product Website address if one is available.


## Social Media Contests

Create a special contest where supporters can sign up through your social media website.  Have friends "like" you through Facebook to get a special coupon that you've created.  This coupon could be for any service (yard mowing, house service, oil change, car washing, etc.)

You may also place coupons through GroupOn.com or Pinterest.com.  These coupons could be for something free that you've already acquired from a local business.

Just be sure that you ask for a legitimate name address, phone number and email address when you offer the item or you will be just wasting your time.

# Future Trends

Much of the future trends in fundraising increasingly involve usage of online technology. In fact, parents of youth conducting a fundraiser are much more likely to support an online fundraising effort by buying items in support of the fundraiser than other local supporters.

This social media trend is increasingly more important as national fundraising companies head in that direction while decreasing actual face-to-face fundraising methods.

Online fundraising is also increasing in frequency, because children and youth are not exposed to unsavory individuals who may not have their best interests in mind.

Another reason online fundraisers are proliferating is that parents have less time available due to stressful careers, so they tend to maximize their time with friends through email, texting and online social media.

You can take these online fundraising programs and direct volunteers and supporters to help with your own fundraising efforts by using their own social media channels to tell others who they know.

You may also look into online fundraising programs like those seen at FreeWebFundraiser.com which require very little volunteers and will still allow you to engage your supporters in helping you raise funds.

**Delivery Of Fundraising Products Straight To The Customer's Home**

There are some exciting trends which are guaranteed to change the fundraising landscape, while eliminating the hassles and time consumption of personally delivering the products by the Fundraising Team Members to their customers.

These trends from fundraising companies are:

- ❖ eCard Sales

- ❖ Online Microsite Sales

- ❖ Online Fundraising With Automated Monthly Sales

I will discuss each here and will list some online product programs that are taking advantage of this trend. Take note of the benefits listed for your convenience.

## eCard Sales

On the outset, the On-The-Spot sale of an eCard rather than an actual product can be offered for practically any product. The eCards are about the size of a credit card and can be sold on-the-spot and later redeemed by the customer online to secure their items of choice.

– Benefits –

- Made for quick On-The-Spot Sales like any merchant card can be offered.
- Fixed sales amount -- Usually $15 to $20 each.
- Redeemable online by the consumer for the exact items they desire. For example, the may choose the exact cookie dough flavor they prefer.
- Items are shipped straight to the customer's home; thereby, avoiding extra time needed to deliver their product by Fundraising Team members.
- eCards can be redeemed immediately after receipt of the card by the customer. This may save 3-4 weeks for delivery time and eliminate

customer frustration that normally comes with traditional delivery of products through the Fundraising Team Member.

- Once the eCard is sold to the customer, no further action is needed by the Fundraising Team Members or the organization. The group may immediately begin using their funds generated. This makes for a fun and easy effort by the whole fundraising team.

– Downside –

- Mostly used for one type of item only. For example cookie dough and candles are an excellent choice for an eCard, but it is not as great for multiple categories of products with multiple pricing that may add unnecessary confusion for the consumer.
- Limited to local sales typically, because you place the card into the hand of the customer immediately via a face-to-face purchase. You may mail the cards at a very low cost, but would need to assume that the card doesn't get "lost in the mail" or you will have to repurchase the card and mail to the customer again. This also assumes that the buyer is trustworthy and simply will not later claim they never received it although some tracking of cards may be available.
- Sold for one fixed price usually. Each card is imprinted at $15 or $20 on its face with a special code identifying the card. To get more products, it requires buying more cards. For instance, if the price on your eCard is $20 and your cookie dough is $12 per tub but the customer wants to purchase two tubs of cookie dough, then the customer will need to buy two $20 cards or would need to pay the difference if offered by the online product company. Forty dollars (2 X $20 card) is more than most people will want to spend on cookie dough so it may become impractical to expect customers to buy more than one tub.
- Overage amounts may occur. For instance, if the price on your eCard is $20 and your cookie dough is $12 per tub, then the remaining $8 will be lost or just can't be used at the moment.

– Program Examples –

Online Cookie Dough Fundraiser – Each eCard sells for $20.00 On-The-Spot or by using a pre-order sales brochure which is valid for cookie dough and many other products. The nonprofit group pays $12 for the card so they make a profit of $8 per card sold.  It allows supporters to redeem the eCards online or by telephone where their order is delivered direct to their own address!

## Online Microsite Sales

Online Microsite Sales is one of the most exciting trends sure to make huge inroads in the near future.

Microsites are easy, powerful and a safe sales method for any group to raise big profits. It allows you to reach across local barriers to gather national supporters.

Basically, a Microsite is given to each Fundraising Team Member or student allowing that person to offer the chosen fundraising products to their friends and family on their own webpage.  They may post their own information like a picture, personal fundraising goal (shown on a thermometer) that is updated in real-time as people they refer buy a product.  They may add a short paragraph of why they are personally involved and helping to raise funds for the group with clickable links to the product purchase webpage.

As supporters get involved through their Microsite and buy a product or service, they receive immediate credit shown on their personal fundraising goal board or on a goal thermometer.  Sometimes the supporters name is also shown indicating how much they helped; thus, encouraging others that may know them to get involved too.

– Benefits –

- Your organization will have no products to handle.  It's all showcased online.
- Shipping is taken care of by the product company, since it is an integrated feature of using an online shopping platform which the customer can access.
- The customer has the convenience of shopping online 24/7, 365 days a year using various means of payment in a secure fashion.
- A fundraising campaign can be started immediately once the online ecommerce store has been created for your organization with your own Fundraising Products Website address.

- Offer an endless variety of products with various pricing already listed on your Microsite and sold through the ecommerce portion of the website.
- The capabilities of online fundraising require no money collection by your members, with no products to handle, and no turn-in-dates to consider.
- The online Product Company processes all sales taxes, shipping. It sends the profits onto a loadable credit card or by check to the nonprofit organization once or twice a month.
- Members can safely reach out to supporters from the comfort of home. No door-to-door selling means an extremely safe fundraising environment for youth, students or Fundraising Team Members.
- Goals and funds raised are automatically updated with each purchase for everyone to see. Usually a Goal Thermometer is shown on the group's Fundraising Product Website (group goal) and the Team Member's Microsite (personal goal).
- Groups can effortlessly generate a personalized fundraising page with their own message, group photos and fundraising goal thermometer fast. This is done much like the social media websites such as Facebook allows. Individual Fundraising Team Members can create their own personal Microsite sub-webpage within the campaign website to promote to their friends, neighbors and relatives asking each to help them reach their personal goal.
- Supporters and friends of Fundraising Team members can also help spread their friend's Microsite webpage by sharing it and inviting others through their Facebook, MySpace, Twitter and LinkedIn accounts.
- Attract supporters through sophisticated marketing and email built into the online system. Some Online Product Companies provide an integrated email marketing program where Fundraising Team Members can invite friends and relatives to participate and spread the word. This is separate from their own email provider. These programs even allow members to easily import their existing contact lists from Hotmail, Gmail, Yahoo, etc. Once friends email addresses have been exported then a series of automated template emails can be sent on the dates you chosen.
- With real time reporting, your Fundraising Campaign Chair can track group sales and generate detailed reports from your Online Campaign Manager provided to your group. This "back office" as it is sometimes called, is your online campaign manager and is password protected

and is meant for use by the Fundraising Campaign Chair and/or key leaders at your organization.

– Downside –

- Not as personal since most of the sales are conducted through online means and not face-to-face.
- The Fundraising Campaign Chair or designee must be able to use internet technology moderately well to manage the campaign online.
- You must use email marketing as your primary means of getting people to each Microsite and purchase a product.

– Program Examples –

Online Products Fundraising Campaign – This includes products from magazines, cookie dough, candy, popcorn, coffee and more. It's much like an online fundraising store.

Premium Popcorn Fundraiser – A nationally known popcorn company has several varieties and flavors of popped popcorn.

Flower/Bulb Fundraiser – Nationally known bulb and flower company provides an easy program for any nonprofit to use. They also provide many marketing resources to help groups reach out to their friends and supporters in the community.

## Online Fundraising With Automated Monthly Sales

How would you like to conduct 12 fundraising sales campaigns all rolled into one? That's right, there are now online automated monthly sales programs that generate 12 times more than normal fundraising campaign profits and come in each and every month of the year by initiating only one fundraising campaign.

How about taking the online Microsite sales platform mentioned earlier and then adding in an automated monthly sales program which processes a standing order and automatically accepts a customer's payment on a monthly basis and then ships their product to their home address? Wouldn't that be the perfect fundraising platform?

These online automated monthly sales programs have been set up by the actual customer at the time of the first sale to automatically draft their banking accounts or credit cards so there is no chance of getting their order wrong.

Many times the customer is given their own Product Managing Website which allows them to change the quantity of products, change the product types, cancel their order, change the shipping date or change payment types as their budget allows.

– Benefits –

- Your Sales Team only sells once, but collects funds all year long.
- There is no delivery of products by your members. It's done for them by the product supplier straight from their warehouse to your supporter's (the customer) home.
- There are no money collecting hassles for your group to mess with since all transactions are handled automatically by the product company. They deal directly with your customer if there is an issue, so your organization doesn't have to spend any extra time on orders.
- Automatic processing each month means automatic funds sent to your group each month without any extra work on your part.
- See additional benefits as previously listed in the Online Microsites Sales section.

– Downside –

- Not as personal since most of the sales are conducted through online means and not face-to-face.
- The Fundraising Campaign Chair or designee must be able to use internet technology moderately well to manage the campaign online.
- You must use email marketing as your primary means of getting people to each Microsite and purchase a product.
- Some customers may find it hard to understand that monthly deductions occur automatically from their financial accounts to cover their monthly product orders. Once set up there is no extra worry on

their part except to keep track of their financial accounts to avoid any overage fees.

Coffee Fundraiser – This fundraiser is much like a Coffee Club program which provides excellent ongoing revenue as orders are automatically generated once a month and shipped straight to the customer.  It can be promoted once or several times throughout the year.


**Direct Sale Companies Offering Fundraising Programs**

Part of the future trends increasingly involves online network marketing companies and direct sales companies entering the fundraising arena.  They are experts at knowing how to market to consumers and how to integrate sales through online technology with direct delivery to the customer's home.

One unique direct sales company offers products or services through an online sales platform provided for the organization at no charge.  The nonprofit receives a portion of the profits each month made from sales generated by their supporters.  Products and services are provided straight to the customer's home without the organization ever needing to do anything except promote their special fundraising website to friends and supporters.  Some examples can be found at FreeWebFundraiser.com.

Your organization may want to evaluate one or more of these companies as you choose a sustainable product to offer your supporters.  Sustainability is the key to long term success.  The company should be offer a credible brand that will establish immediate confidence to your supporters about your efforts.

It ultimately comes down to how the company treats potential customers (your supporters).   Here is a quick guide when evaluating network marketing companies or direct sales companies offering a nonprofit or fundraising program (sometimes called a "Gives Back" Program).

- Beware of those charging any fees for website hosting, mandatory large product buys, processing fees, or costs for start-up kits.  If everything is free to participate, as a nonprofit organization would expect to receive, then you can proceed into reviewing their products further.  There's no reason for any nonprofit group to "spend money to make money" through these companies. If any fees crop up, don't just walk away from those companies... run away.

- Sometimes big names attract attention to your fundraiser and can be of value. You don't have to explain the products from companies like Tupperware®, Mary Kay®, Scentsy® Candles, or other big names, because the name says it all.

- Some companies only "give back" a portion of all sales to a particular organization they've chosen corporately (which you may not agree with supporting) or may they offer a portion of the sales commissions back through its Affiliates who in turn passes on a donation to the local organization. I prefer those that have an automated payment system straight from the corporate bank account.

- Direct Sales companies may ideally offer an effective means for individuals who need long term funding for personal, medical or children's activities. These individuals may be required to pay for multiple pageants, foreign language trips, student ambassador programs, medical costs, missionary trips, or saving for an adoption.

- Income from fundraising sales, made through these companies, require payment of income taxes unless your group is tax exempt. Find out if they accept your tax exempt documentation [IRS 501(c)3 letter] in order to set up a nonprofit fundraising website for your group. You may also need to apply for an EIN found at IRS.gov.

- Sometimes it's a Distributor, Affiliate or Representative of a direct sale company who, in turn, personally donates funds back to the group as your group fundraiser attracts new customers for them. This is OK only if helping out a friend or relative you trust. For instance Tupperware® sales conducted in a Distributor's home you are familiar with, for the benefit of a church youth group, would be acceptable since the youth group is not bound by any agreements from the company. Find out how your group is paid for your efforts in promoting their products.

- When any of your supporters buy from a direct sales company, keep in mind that they will also become the customer of that company. Determine if this is acceptable for your group.

- If the company is essentially a "recruitment mill", where its main objective is to recruit people; rather than strictly selling a good product or service, then you should avoid associating with them outright. This mandatory focus on recruitment of individuals is often referred to as a "pyramid scheme", because it is building a pyramid of distributors as its main function. Keep in mind, while selling products, you may reasonably expect to increase sales by recruiting your own helpers, sometimes called Independent Business Owners, through the company business building system. This can also be called a Referral System paying your group for helping get the word out further by allowing your customers to also benefit financially. This is a perfectly acceptable and reasonable way of increasing awareness and profits.

These are just a few areas of thought you need to review before working with any fundraising program offered by any Network Marketing Company or Direct Sale Company.

– Program Examples –

Online Social Commerce Fundraiser – A unique social membership program provides automated monthly income from sales of products or services that the consumer already uses like electricity, cellular service, insurance, major retail stores, and more. It provides a free website for the nonprofit organizations. The great part of this program is that once the customer signs up the nonprofit gets permanent credit anytime that customer places an order. These orders could be placed multiple times during the month meaning more profits coming in.

**Helping You Succeed Is My Goal**

I hope that this book has been a valuable addition to you and your organization's fundraising efforts. Fundraising is a very dynamic and personal type activity. Each nonprofit group... each volunteer... every donor... all supporters each bring in their own personality to the total picture creating a wonderful tapestry of charitable good works.

This brings to mind that your fundraising campaign may be slightly different than the exact details outlined in this book, so I would encourage you to adapt it to your own unique personalities involved.

I would caution you from expecting these exact plans to exactly fit with your group's method of conducting a fundraiser, but mostly it will do nicely.

These fundraising principles are proven and will create a reliable source of funding should you heed them. I wish you great success with all of your endeavors.

# Tools And Forms

Fundraising Introductory Letter From Nonprofit Members To Friends

Key Leader's Kickoff Letter (sometimes called Parent's Letter)

Job Description – Fundraising Committee Chair

Job Description – Fundraising Committee Member

Job Description – Fundraising Campaign Chair

Job Description – Fundraising Team Leader

Job Description – Fundraising Team Member

Walk-A-Thon Sponsor Sign Up Form

Preferred Fundraising Product - Survey Form

Thermometer Goal Charts – By Financial Goal or By Participation Goal

A Checklist For Success

**Other Forms Not Included In This Book That You May Need** –These and
other forms can be downloaded for your use free at
FundraisingYourWay.com.

- Typical Campaign Guidelines
- Fundraising Sales Order Form
- Final Order Form
- Thank You Letters
- Parent's Letters
- Kickoff Notifications Forms

**Fundraising Introductory Letter From Nonprofit Members To Friends**

*(Your contact information goes here or use your group's letterhead)*

Dear _____:

I'm reaching out to you and a few of my friends and relatives in hopes that you will help me reach my personal goal in a fundraiser I'm presently involved with.

I am part of the fundraising team for *(you nonprofit group name goes here)* and I am very excited about this new fundraiser we've kicked off and I wanted to give everyone I know the opportunity to participate with me.

I am hoping you will be one of 5 people who will help me successfully reach my personal goal. Our fundraiser is offering *(product selection goes here)* from our group's fundraising brochure seen here (*post the PDF online link or fundraising website here*).

Our organization's goal is to raise $_____ to help *(what you're needing money for goes here)*.

We've been asked to wrap up our fundraiser by *(put your completion date here)* where I will be able to announce my 100% Goal Completion to our team.

I hope that I can count on your participation to help me reach my goal.

Be sure to also share our fundraising information or website with as many people as you know. It sure will help us.

Feel free to email me or call me anytime at ( _____ ) _____-_____ with your questions. I'll also try to reach out to you soon. Have a great day.

Sincerely,

*(sign here)*

Your Name
Fundraising Team Member
*(Your email address here)*

## *Key Leader's Kickoff Letter (sometimes called Parent's Letter)*

Dear Parents:

I wanted to be the first to let you know that the **ABC School PTO** has just kicked off its fundraising campaign. I'm serving as the Chair of this campaign and have the responsibility to ask that you and your student help us out as one of our Fundraising Team Members.

Our Principal _____, has given us the "green light" to conduct this totally unique product fundraiser that I believe you will be excited about.

Basically, we've partnered with a fundraising company called _____ that has been in business for many years and our goal we plan on reaching is $_____ to help supply our students with_____.

We are expecting 100% participation from our student families and I am asking for your careful consideration to support our efforts.  You can help us by...

1. Reviewing the accompanying fundraising brochure and make a selection yourself first before asking others.
2. Take your fundraising brochure and gather orders with payment from friends, family, and co-workers.  No COD's please.
3. Return all monies and order forms by the end of our Turn-In Date _____.

Every item purchased helps us raise funds.  The suggested personal goal is $_____ per student.  That's just _____ items sold.

I want you to pay particular attention to our Sales Incentive Program that we've designed to show our appreciation for your efforts. *Here they are:*
- ✓ Selling 20 items – you receive a _____.
- ✓ The Top Seller will receive a _____.
- ✓ Early Bird Drawing Held Each Day Of The First Week – You Could Win one of _____.
- ✓ Reach Your Personal Goal And Your Name Will Be Entered In The Weekly Prize Drawing where you could walk away with _____.
- ✓ Every class with 100% student participation will have a _____ party. And please don't forget to view our fundraising website (*if your group has one*).  Post our website address on your social media outlets and email all of your friends to help our organization reach its fundraising goal, simply by going online and shopping at www._____ (*or reviewing a PDF of the product brochure posted online*).

I hope that I can count on your participation with us.  Let your child's Teacher or Room Parent know if you have any questions.  Thanks again for your support.

Sincerely,
ABC School PTO Fundraising Chair

189

## Job Description – Fundraising Committee Chair

As the head of the Fundraising Committee for your organization, you will have the following responsibilities as the top leader of all fundraising activities:

**General Responsibilities:**

To support and assist the Fundraising Campaign Chair who you've recruited for your organization as it involves any given fundraising campaign during the year and to work with that Fundraising Campaign Chair in enlisting other individuals to help, as necessary, in order to be successful.

**Specific Responsibilities:**

1. Give direction to the overall fundraising strategy for your organization.
2. Understand the Fundraising Your Way (FundraisingYourWay.net) fundraising book thoroughly.
3. Conduct fundraising strategy sessions with your Fundraising Committee monthly or quarterly as needed.
4. Set the example and purchase your own products during any fundraising effort and become a customer yourself first before asking others to do so.
5. Ask for feedback regularly from your fundraising committee and any Fundraising Campaign Chair you've recruited.
6. Work with members of your committee to recruit volunteers (Fundraising Campaign Chair) and fundraising workers as needed for the overall nonprofit fundraising program.
7. Assign specific responsibilities to each member of the Fundraising Committee as needed.
8. Constantly evaluate goals and adjust when necessary.
9. Steer the Fundraising Committee to set priorities, policies, and goals for the year.

**Suggestions To Make Your Job Easier:**

- Be accessible to the members of the Fundraising Committee.
- Work closely with your Fundraising Campaign Chair to implement marketing and promotional strategies for any specific fundraising campaign or effort.
- Familiarize yourself with any fundraising websites, fundraising literature and nonprofit fundraising management tools as thoroughly as possible.

## Job Description – Fundraising Committee Member

As a member of the Fundraising Committee, you will have the following responsibilities:

### General Responsibilities:

To support and assist the Fundraising Committee Chair and any Fundraising Campaign Chair recruited for your organization involving any specified fundraising emphasis during the year.

### Specific Responsibilities:

1. Work with the Fundraising Committee Chair and accept responsibilities as assigned to you and help successfully implement the fundraising program.
2. Set the example and purchase your own products during any fundraising effort and become a customer yourself first before asking others to do so. Participate at the highest level possible which will inspire others to do the most possible.
3. Realize this as a very worthwhile endeavor and that the Fundraising Committee Chair and Fundraising Campaign Chair depend on your timely completion of tasks assigned. In order to succeed, your complete support, commitment, and involvement will be appreciated.
4. Work with the Fundraising Committee Chair to constantly evaluate your group's fundraising goals and adjust when necessary.
5. Be on the lookout for other non-members that may be interested in participating with your group's fundraising efforts in some manner. Bring their names to the attention of the Fundraising Committee Chair immediately.
6. Assist the Fundraising Committee Chair to set fundraising priorities, policies, and goals throughout the year.

### Suggestions To Make Your Job Easier:

o If you have questions, concerns or need help, then don't hesitate to reach out to your Fundraising Committee Chair.
o Familiarize yourself with any fundraising websites and fundraising books (like the one at FundraisingYourWay.net) as thoroughly as possible.

# Job Description – Fundraising Campaign Chair

As a member of the Fundraising Committee for a specified timeframe or on an annual basis, you will have the following responsibilities: *Also for use by any Division Chair within larger campaigns.*

## General Responsibilities:

To be the "Point Person" responsible for promoting and facilitating the marketing plan of your organization's product fundraising program you were specifically recruited to lead.

## Specific Responsibilities:

1. Thoroughly understand the contents of the Fundraising Your Way fundraising book (www.FundraisingYourWay.net).
2. Help set the example as your group's main Fundraising Leader and become the first customer to purchase fundraising products during any fundraising effort before asking others to do so.
3. Make regular reports to the Fundraising Committee about the progress of the fundraising campaign and enlist their help through the Fundraising Committee Chair as needed.
4. Plan and implement the fundraising campaign with enough Team Members recruited to successfully complete the campaign and reach the set goal.
5. Advise the Fundraising Committee consistently and evaluate the final outcome of the fundraising campaign. Stress areas that need improvement.
6. Properly acknowledge all Fundraising Team Members who worked during the fundraising campaign.

## Suggestions To Make Your Job Easier:

- Familiarize yourself with any fundraising websites and fundraising materials as thoroughly as possible.
- Regularly ask for and review reports of how your fundraising campaign is progressing from the Division Chairs, Fundraising Team Leaders and Fundraising Team Members.

# Job Description – Fundraising Team Leader

As a Team Leader of the Fundraising Campaign, you will have the following responsibilities: Use the term *Division Chair* in place of Campaign Chair for larger campaigns.

## General Responsibilities:

To assist the Fundraising Campaign Chair in an efficient manner completing tasks on time and reporting the results as required while supporting the Fundraising Team Members on your team.

## Specific Responsibilities:

1. Work with the Fundraising Campaign Chair and accept responsibilities as assigned to complete the specific fundraising campaign successfully.
2. Set the example and purchase your own products during any fundraising effort and become a customer yourself first before asking supporters, friends, relatives, neighbors or any Fundraising Team Member to do so. Participate at the highest level possible which will inspire others to do the most possible themselves.
3. Realize this as a very worthwhile endeavor and that your Fundraising Campaign Chair depends on your timely completion of tasks assigned. In order to succeed, your complete support, commitment, and involvement is necessary. Attend all training and kickoff meetings. Encourage your Team Members to turn in orders and money on time at the Due Date.
4. Be on the lookout for other non-members that may be interested in participating with your group's fundraising efforts in some manner. Immediately bring their names to the attention of your Fundraising Campaign Chair.
5. Deliver all products purchased from you by your customers (supporters) in a timely manner. When delivering, do not leave items out in the weather or on a porch where they could be stolen or taken by an animal.
6. Treat your customers with utmost respect and give them plenty of time to consider their purchases. Accept the whole payment at the time of purchase and do not accept CODs. Thank customers at every opportunity for their support.

## Suggestions To Make Your Job Easier:

o If you have questions, concerns or need help, then don't hesitate to reach out to your Fundraising Committee Chair.
o Familiarize yourself with any fundraising materials and brochures given to you as thoroughly as possible (see FundraisingYourWay.net).

# Job Description – Fundraising Team Member

As a Team Member of the Fundraising Campaign, you will have the following responsibilities:

## General Responsibilities:

To support and assist your Fundraising Team Leader and Fundraising Campaign Chair in an efficient manner completing tasks on time and reporting the results as required.

## Specific Responsibilities:

1. Work with the Fundraising Team Leader and accept responsibilities as assigned to successfully complete the specific fundraising campaign.
2. Set the example and purchase your own products during any fundraising effort and become a customer yourself first before asking supporters, friends, relatives and neighbors to do so. Participate at the highest level possible which will inspire others to do the most possible themselves.
3. Realize this as a very worthwhile endeavor and that your Fundraising Team Leader and Fundraising Campaign Chair depend on your timely completion of tasks assigned. In order to succeed, your complete support, commitment, and involvement is appreciated. Attend all training and kickoff meetings. Turn in orders and money on time by the Due Date.
4. Be on the lookout for other non-members that may be interested in participating with your group's fundraising efforts in some manner. Immediately bring their names to the attention of your Fundraising Team Leader or the Fundraising Campaign Chair.
5. Deliver all products purchased from you by your customers (supporters) in a timely manner. When delivering, do not leave items out in the weather or on a porch where they could be stolen or taken by an animal.
6. Treat your customers with utmost respect and give them plenty of time to consider their purchases. Accept the whole payment at the time of purchase and do not accept CODs. Thank customers at every opportunity for their support.

## Suggestions To Make Your Job Easier:

o If you have questions, concerns or need help, then don't hesitate to reach out to your Fundraising Team Leader.
o Familiarize yourself with any fundraising materials and brochures given to you as thoroughly as possible (see FundraisingYourWay.net).

# Walk-A-Thon Sponsor Form

Organization / School / Church _____

Organization Goal $ _____ Walk-A-Thon Participant's Name _____

Your email _____ Phone #_____

Team Leader's Name _____ Phone#_____

Make Checks Payable To: _____(our organization)

Dear Potential Sponsor: I am participating in the Walk-A-Thon for our organization. Proceeds will help fund our activities for this year. You can sponsor me for one or more sponsorships. One Walk Sponsorship is $15.00. One Event Sponsorship is $30.00. After the Walk-A-Thon, I will return to tell you how I fared in completing my walk and offer you a special "Thank You" item. Federal law states that this particular contribution is not applicable for a tax deduction. We appreciate your support.

| Sponsor's Name | Address, City, State, Zip, Phone | No. of Sponsor -ships | X $30 ea. X $15 ea. | TOTAL |
|---|---|---|---|---|
|  |  |  |  |  |
|  |  |  |  |  |
|  |  |  |  |  |
|  |  |  |  |  |
|  |  |  |  |  |
|  |  |  |  |  |
|  |  |  | **Page Total** |  |

Participants: To reach our goal, we ask each participant to find 7 Sponsors. Please bring this form to _____ (location) at the walk-a-thon day, _____ (Day of the Week), _____ (Date).

Tips on making your sponsorship effort a success: Always act in a courteous and polite manner. Make a list of potential sponsors you wish to call before proceeding. Ask friends, relatives, and neighbors for their sponsorship. Please print clearly on the form. Children or youth should never fundraise door-to-door without adult supervision. Adults/Parents please help by taking this form to your workplace and posting in their social media.

# Preferred Fundraising Product - Survey Form

We need your help in selecting our next product fundraiser and your input is invaluable. Please fill out this form and send it to:

_____

Group Name_____ Today's Date _____
Person Filling Out Form_____ Phone Number_____
Email Address _____

## Past Successful Fundraising Events:

| Year Raised | Product | No. Helpers | Amt. Sold | % Profit | Total |
|---|---|---|---|---|---|
| ____ | _____ | _____ | _____ | _____ | _____ |
| ____ | _____ | _____ | _____ | _____ | _____ |
| ____ | _____ | _____ | _____ | _____ | _____ |
| ____ | _____ | _____ | _____ | _____ | _____ |

(If multiple events were held in the same year use a separate line for each event including time of year if other than the fall season.) List any specific comments about each on the back of this form.

## List of products/events currently being considered by us:

_____
_____

## Products/Events held in our area by other organizations:

| Group | Product | Time Of Year | Success ? * | Duplication Y/N? |
|---|---|---|---|---|
| _____ | _____ | _____ | _____ | _____ |
| _____ | _____ | _____ | _____ | _____ |
| _____ | _____ | _____ | _____ | _____ |

(*Levels of Success: 1. Not at all, 2. Min $, 3. Fairly successful, 4. Successful, 5. Huge success)

## Your Top 5 Suggestions (fill in as complete as possible)

| Rank | Product Type | %Profit | Profit/Item | # Participants Needed | Goal/ Member | Profit Potential |
|---|---|---|---|---|---|---|
| ____ | _____ | _____ | _____ | _____ | _____ | _____ |
| ____ | _____ | _____ | _____ | _____ | _____ | _____ |
| ____ | _____ | _____ | _____ | _____ | _____ | _____ |
| ____ | _____ | _____ | _____ | _____ | _____ | _____ |

## Other fundraisers you or your friends feel should be considered:

_____

Once the top five have been selected, submit your survey to the Campaign Chair who will call the distributor or supplier and discuss getting started with the top choice from all surveys. Ideally, whichever profit potential is greatest, that should be the preferred product type. Final selection will be dependent on the kind of group represented. For instance, don't expect a group of young boys on a baseball team to sell jewelry items even if there is a large profit potential available.

# Financial Goal

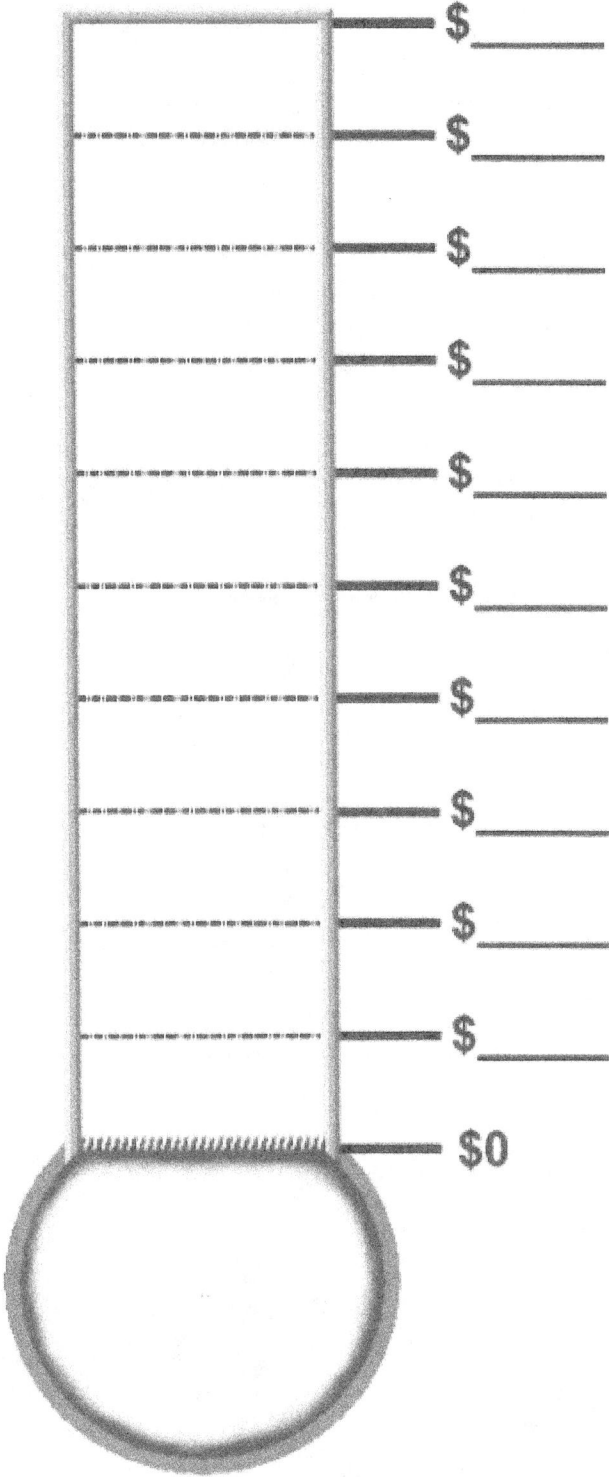

$ _____

$ _____

$ _____

$ _____

$ _____

$ _____

$ _____

$ _____

$ _____

$ _____

$0

# Participation Goal

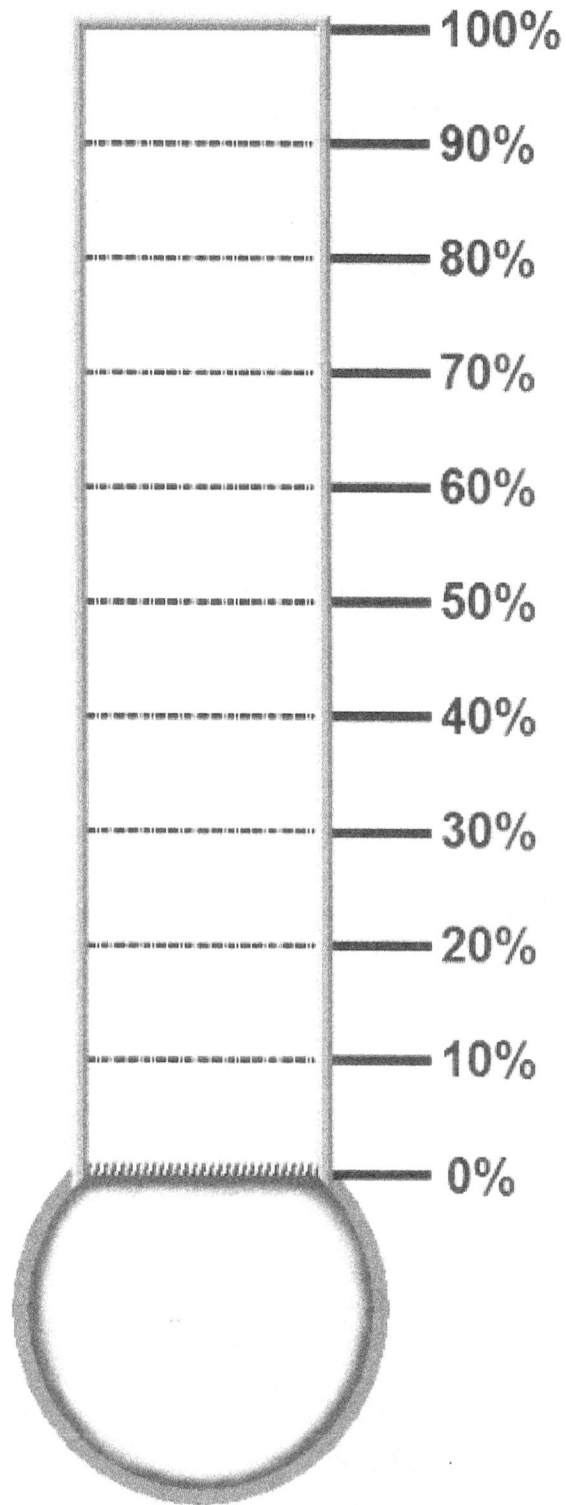

100%

90%

80%

70%

60%

50%

40%

30%

20%

10%

0%

# Checklist For Success

This section provides a checklist of steps needed to roll-out a successful Product Fundraising Program. For more details on each you will need to review the appropriate section in this book.

✓ Make sure you are familiar with the information and material in this book.

✓ Get the approval from your Key Leadership Committee or Board to conduct a product fundraiser. Select your Campaign Kickoff Date and Length of campaign. Have a set fundraising goal. This will help you determine how many Fundraising Team Members you will need in order to reach that goal.

✓ Select your fundraising products of choice and determine who the Target Customer Base is that your group will be approaching.

✓ Choose your fundraising supplier or distributor who offers your selected fundraising product. With your Fundraising Distributor or Product Supplier determine profit you'll receive, pricing, shipping, handling, forms to use, timeframes, payment methods and other campaign details. Discuss the various methods of sales used: Sales Brochures of Flyers, On-The-Spot Sales, or Fundraising Website Sales.

✓ Recruit Your Team - Select your Campaign Chair, Fundraising Team Leaders, Fundraising Team Members and Committee Chairs if needed. Train them and make sure they understand the sales timeframe, payment methods you accept, turn-in procedures for order forms and payments, pickup dates and procedures for redistribution of products to customers.

✓ Decide on the methods you will publicize and promote your fundraising campaign to your members, supporters and throughout your community. Promote your fundraiser and sales timeframe to your community through posters, flyers, social media, emails, banners, website, cell phone texts, and TV or radio announcements.

✓ Be prepared to answer any questions from people in your community that are considering buying or becoming involved.

✓ Get every Key Leader, Fundraising Team Leader and Fundraising Team Member in your organization on board as a Customer first before asking others. This shows that your Team Leaders and Team Members are 100% on board and that they are "leading by example". It sets a strong pace for your fundraiser as you begin. Then, initiate an invitation to your general membership and community supporters. Suggest that Team Members write down a list (parents, grandparents, aunts, uncles, relatives, co-workers, religious worship group, neighbors, friends, work associates, vendors) of possible customers before proceeding with their efforts.

✓ Continually update your Fundraising Team Members with the progress of your fundraising campaign, timelines and announcement of any positive results of your fundraiser. Actively highlight those individuals that have achieved personal sales incentives that you offer so that others will be more inclined to achieving them as well.

✓ Be sure to deposit all retail funds collected after the Turn In Date and process your final order with your fundraising distributor as quickly as possible. Double check your orders while delaying only long enough to give a few days leeway for possible late orders. Secure an approximate arrival date of your products from your fundraising distributor or supplier and start making plans for distributing the products back through your Fundraising Team Members to your Supporters.

✓ Have your Fundraising Team Members pick up items at your prescribed Pick Up Date and location. Stress to Team Members that the items should take no more than a week to be delivered to customers. An alternate method would be to have a "pick up" date where items can be picked up by the customers themselves. Include a "Thank You" card or flyer with each delivery thanking them for their assistance or you may also thank them personally by telephone.

✓ Conclude with recognition of participation and key achievements of all Fundraising Team Members to all other members and throughout the community. Distribute any prizes and sales incentives in a timely manner realizing that your Fundraising Team Members were the KEY to success. Tell your community of the success that was achieved though news media, email and social media.

✓ Develop a system for use so that next year you will have an archive and complete record of your fundraising campaign activities, customers and volunteers. Build on that success and the customer base to make your next year even more of an achievement.

## NOW, for New Fundraising Product Customers…

As a way of thanking you for purchasing my book… *Fundraising Your Way: How To Conduct An Effective And Profitable Product Fundraiser*, I want to help you out even more with a special bargain.

**Start any one of our Select Fundraisers and use the $30 Retail Gift Certificate to get any qualifying item you want absolutely FREE!**

Make a copy of this page and clip the coupon and send in with your Final Order Form after completing one of our selected fundraising programs and your free items will be included with the order.  This coupon can only be used for Qualified Fundraising Products (QFP) as posted on the Fundraising Products page seen at **ProfitQuests.com** and **FundraisingYourWay.com**.

Your free items must be of the same type as the order you send in.  For example, if you ordered Finest Fragrance Candles, then your free items must be any one of the scented candles of your choice.  If you have two different product lines being conducted at the same time and turned them in together, you may select from each category until your $30 retail value has been met.

You can then turn around and sell your free items for pure profit; give them away as incentives to your Top Sales People, Campaign Team Leaders, The Top Performing Teacher; or keep them for yourself (the Fundraising Campaign Chair) as a special "thank you" from us for a job well done.  It's your choice.  *If you don't use this offer, get with your own Fundraising Company for their own "sign on" specials.*

---

# FREE  $30 Gift Certificate

*Used toward the purchase of any fundraising product item at the RETAIL price from any qualifying fundraiser you've conducted at:*

**www.ProfitQuests.com**   OR   **www.FundraisingYourWay.com**

Qualifying Fundraising Product programs are shown at each website on the Fundraising Products page and labeled as:  **QFP**
***This certificate must accompany your order.***

*Offer valid for buyers of* **Fundraising Your Way** *books by Jesse Carter.  There is no cash value for this certificate and it cannot be used for any other purpose (like shipping, handing or any other costs) than to secure the actual product items. This is for a One-Time use only for first time customers and any remaining retail dollar value remaining may not be used toward other purchases at a later time. Valid for organizations in Continental USA only.*

---

www.ingramcontent.com/pod-product-compliance
Lightning Source LLC
Chambersburg PA
CBHW051213200326
41519CB00025B/7095